# DESTINATION
# *Chesapeake*

## 15 Great Cruises in
## MARYLAND

From the editors of *Chesapeake Bay Magazine*—
Wendy Mitman Clarke
Ann Levelle
T. F. Sayles
Jody Argo Schroath

CHESAPEAKE BAY MEDIA
601 Sixth Street
Annapolis, Maryland 21403

# TABLE OF CONTENTS

Havre de Grace •

• Bohemia River

• Sassafras River

Middle River •

Patpapsco River •

Severn River •

Annapolis •

• Kent Island

• St. Michaels
• Easton
• Oxford

• Dorchester County

Patuxent River •

St. Mary's City •

• Crisfield

# PREFACE

It is with both pleasure and pride that I welcome you to *Chesapeake Bay Magazine*'s first book, a very generous baker's dozen (fifteen) of our favorite Maryland boating destination articles from the past decade. Why only Maryland? Simple: It's a great big Bay, and we had to find *some* way to divide it up into manageable book-size pieces. When in doubt, Ptolemy would insist, go with geography. So this time around we keep our focus north of the maritime state line, which zigzags across the middle Bay from Smith Point to the Pocomoke River. Next up is a Virginia version of this book, coming your way in time for Christmas.

The anonymous quotation on the page that follows this preface, often incorrectly attributed to Mark Twain, wisely warns us that we will come to regret more keenly the things we have not done than things we have done. It is perhaps the most appropriate choice for this book—especially the bit about throwing off the bow lines and setting sail. But it is actually not my favorite pearl of wisdom on the subject of travel. That would be one that does indeed come from the incomparable Sam Clemens. "Travel is fatal to prejudice, bigotry and narrow-mindedness, and many of our people need it sorely on these accounts," he wrote. "Broad, wholesome, charitable views of men and things cannot be acquired by vegetating in one little corner of the earth all one's lifetime."

It was many years ago when I first read those words in Twain's 1869 book *Innocents Abroad*, which, not unlike this volume, was a compilation of articles written for newspapers in San Francisco and New York. But clearly the idea stayed with me. Who knows, maybe it was the very thing that pointed me, ultimately if not immediately, in the direction of travel writing. And maybe it explains why I always feel somehow *improved* when I return from a trip to a wholly new place—not improved in the sense of being a better person, of course, but rather of having an ever-so-slightly more accurate and nuanced conception of the world, if only that one little corner of it.

If I may be so cheeky as to edit Twain, I would add misconception and simplism to the list of things to which travel is fatal. It has long been a habit of mine, a sort of pastime in the immediate aftermath of a trip, to compare what had been my mental picture of a place (or thing or institution or even body of water) to the actual place or thing. This can be tricky, because reality—seeing something with your own eyes—can very quickly ink over the pencil sketch that had been your preconception. But sometimes, if you work at it, you can still make out the faint lines and shapes of your unschooled notions, and compare them to the freshly installed reality. Perhaps I am too easily amused, but I find it an excellent cure for the blues of a long, anticlimactic voyage home.

That calls to mind another Mark Twain pearl, from an 1883 letter to his boyhood friend, Will Bowen: "There is no unhappiness like the misery of sighting land (and work) again after a cheerful, careless voyage."

May you enjoy the cheerful, careless voyages that follow, and may you find that they improve you.

—*T. F. Sayles, editor,* Chesapeake Bay Magazine*, September 2014*

*Twenty years from now you will be more disappointed by the things you did not do than by the things you did do. So throw off the bow lines, sail away from the safe harbor. Catch the trade winds in your sails. Explore. Dream. Discover.*
—Anonymous

*Havre de Grace:*

# 1

## The Great Havre de Grace Culture Clash

*Can three friends visit one Havre de Grace museum for every restaurant they visit? It's more than a city's culture that gets weighed in the balance!*

*by Jody Argo Schroath*

If you want to talk people into coming up the Bay to visit four museums in two days, you'd better have the right stick and julienned carrot. "I'm sailing up to Havre de Grace next week," I began, when my daughter Colby, good friend Kathy and I were gathered one weekend. "Come on up and visit me. There are some nice little museums there I want to see."

This was the stick, and it was met with the anticipated reaction, which is to say, none. But then I waved the carrot: "And I thought that each time we visited a museum, we'd reward ourselves by then eating at one of Havre de Grace's dozen or so nice restaurants." That did it.

"Oh . . . well, that might be fun," Colby said.

"How . . . big are these museums?" Kathy asked.

"Big enough so that you can work up an appetite between meals, but not so big that you'll starve," I assured her. She was in too—I knew my audience. So I outlined my plan, and we set the date. I would bring *Moment of Zen* up during the week from Annapolis, and they would drive up to meet me over the weekend and stay on the boat. On Saturday we'd visit a museum, go to lunch, visit another museum and go to dinner. The following day we'd repeat the process. In between, we'd walk around, exploring the town. Then they'd go home, and I'd continue my cruise. Perfect.

The following week, I set my part of the plan into action. Accompanied by Skipper, the ship's dog and docking consultant, I left Port Annapolis Marina on a Thursday in mid-July, motoring across a glassy, windless harbor. Above the Chesapeake Bay Bridge, the morning wind piped up, and I soon had the sails up and the motors off. On light winds we ghosted past Rock Hall, Swan Creek and Tolchester. We had just passed Fairlee Creek when the wind slackened and then petered out altogether. I drifted into Still Pond on the last of it and dropped anchor not far from the entrance to the creek.

The next morning, Skipper and I sailed and then motored the rest of the way up to Havre de Grace, cutting west near the entrance to Elk Creek to follow the deep and well-marked channel around the edge of the Susquehanna Flats to reach town. On previous occasions, I had stayed at the city Yacht Basin and at Tidewater Marina, so I had decided to stop at Log Pond on this visit. All of Havre de Grace's marinas are convenient to town, from town dock on the south to Havre de Grace Marina on the north. It's one of the town's many charms that it's so easy to get to by boat and to get around once you are docked.

Havre de Grace Marina at Log Pond (its official name) is located behind a condominium complex, just south of Tidewater Marina. The docks are older but floating, which is always nice. With Skipper barking directions to me from his position aft, I docked *Zen* at the shore end of the long main pier, which made for a short walk ashore. And since everyone had to walk by the boat to get to or from their boats, I met a lot of people during my stay. Or rather Skipper did. They would stop to talk to him as he kept an eye on things, and then I would show up to keep up our end of the conversation. As a social ploy, it worked pretty well.

The first to fall into my trap were Ivan (a Cape Dory) and Jerry (a trawler named *Whole Lotta Love*), both of whom have kept their boats at Log Pond for years but don't actually live in Havre de Grace. (In fact, no one I met seems to actually live in Havre de Grace.) "I'm looking for some culinary advice," I said as an opening gambit. I needed to do some quick decision-making about where to eat in the weekend's museum/food marathon. Havre de Grace is positively littered with good and interesting restaurants, so how else would I decide? Ask the people who live here, of course—or at least the people who eat here. Ivan and Jerry were simply the first victims. Their answer: Price's Seafood. "It's the only place we ever go, so we don't know about any of the others," they said. Well, I thought, I have one.

Then the choice for a second restaurant was made for me, because someone took me there . . . and, here's the bonus . . . did so after a visit to a museum we were going to visit, the Havre de Grace Maritime Museum. It came about this way: The museum had recently acquired a charming little shad shanty and were keen on learning about the history of shanties—or fishing arks, as they are also called—and looking for funding for restoring theirs. Museum Board of Director's treasurer Toni Bench happened on a story I'd written several years ago on arks, and emailed me for information. Despite the fact that I wasn't much help, she offered to give me a tour of the museum when I was in town, which I was. So that's how I ended up visiting the first museum before Colby and Kathy had even arrived, and got a restaurant thrown in too, which meant I had to consider it part of the weekend package.

*The remains of the Havre de Grace end of the 19th-century Susquehanna and Tidewater Canal, which paralleled the Susquehanna all the way to Wrightsville, Pa., east of York. Preceding pages: Havre de Grace's iconic 1827 Concord Point Lighthouse.*

One of the things I especially like about Havre de Grace's museums—which I'm not going to describe in great detail in this story, since I think a good part of visiting a museum is the discovery of what you didn't know you wanted to see—is that they all give you something special, something you won't find elsewhere. For example, the largest of the four, the Havre de Grace Decoy Museum, while featuring more than a thousand wildfowl decoys by the Bay's most famous carvers (the Ward brothers, Charlie Bryan, Evans McKinney, etc.), also features an exact reproduction of an A. Aubrey Bodine photograph in the form of a "talking" life-size tableau of several famous Havre de Grace decoy carvers gathered around a woodstove. The whole thing is both riveting and spooky. You don't find that kind of thing just anywhere. And although neither can boast its own talking tableaux, the Concord Point Lighthouse and Keepers Dwelling and the Susquehanna Museum at the Lock House are also unique on the Chesapeake.

All of this is particularly true of the Havre de Grace Maritime Museum, which offers bite-size exhibits of Bay history that I have never seen in any other Bay maritime museums—not that I've seen them all yet, though I'm working at it. The museum has fascinating exhibits on Coast Guard safety equipment, ice harvesting on the Susquehanna (once very big business), and the decimation of the waterfowl population in the Susquehanna Flats by large-scale hunting methods (kind of the "yin" to the Decoy Museum's uncritical duck-hunting "yang").

After the tour, I had dinner with Toni Bench and several other museum board members at Tidewater Grille—which made nearly everyone's list in my informal name-the-best-four restaurant poll. The Tidewater Grille is also the only Havre de Grace restaurant that has its own dock so you can boat in for dinner. Its décor is light, airy and open, and the service is friendly and fast. There is a wall of windows that looks out on the Susquehanna bridges and the Flats. I ordered jambalaya, which was loaded with shellfish, chicken and Andouille sausage and spicy enough to make a Cajun cry. Others at the table had blackened mako shark, flat-iron steak, and linguini and clams, among other things I can't remember because I was concentrating on not spontaneously combusting from my jambalaya. It was a lovely meal, and we talked about fishing arks.

Back at the boat, Skipper and I set off for a long walk through town. Log Pond Marina is located about equidistant from Millard E. Tydings Park and three of the town's four museums, as well as the main business district with its restaurants and shops. Havre de Grace is a marvelous hodgepodge of architectural styles, from 1950s storefront to 1890s High Victorian houses—and everything in between. The main business streets are bordered by lovely tree-lined neighborhoods and book-ended north and south by parks that border the water. And its inhabitants are friendly to a fault. As Skipper and I walked through the long summer twilight, we never had to wait for cars to cross the street; they invariably stopped to let us go first.

The next day, Colby and her dog Lacey were the first to arrive, so she and I got right to work. Leaving the dogs on the boat, we walked south along Concord Street to the Decoy Museum, just off the city's promenade, which meanders along the waterfront from Tydings Park to Concord Point Lighthouse. We spent an hour absorbed by exhibits on duck punts, punt guns, sneak boxes (boats that sat so low in the water they were undetectable to waterfowl) and myriad other duck-hunting paraphernalia. And by decoys, dazzling in their craftsmanship and variety. And, of course, the aforementioned talking decoy-maker tableau. When we had finished our tour and reemerged into the summer sunshine, Colby said, "Let's not have anything related to birds for lunch." I agreed, and we set off for downtown. We had no sooner started than we decided to detour to the lighthouse and keepers house, since it was practically next door. As a bonus, Colby pointed out, that would at least earn us a dessert.

The Concord Point Lighthouse is the oldest continuously operating lighthouse in Maryland. It is also an unusually handy one to visit because it sits not only on land but right in the middle of town. Built of local granite in 1827 by John Donahoo, the light was manned by the city's own War of 1812 war hero, John O'Neill. Perhaps you've heard of the brave Irishman who kept firing a heavy cannon at the invading British long after his fellow militiamen had retreated. That was O'Neill. He was captured but soon released by the Brits, and after the war, the story goes, he was rewarded with lifetime employment as lighthouse keeper, and a member of each succeeding generation of O'Neill served as keeper as long as the light was manually lit. The lighthouse was decommissioned in 1975 and now belongs to the city of Havre de Grace. The keeper's house, built at the same time and also of granite, sits behind the lighthouse and has been restored, leaving the original roof line visible from the outside. Both are open to visitors, though in truth, the telling of the lighthouse's story takes longer than the visit.

"A dessert-size museum," Colby said, as we set out once more for lunch. I pointed out that Kathy had better get here soon because we were clicking off museums at top speed. At Girard Street, we cut over two blocks to Washington Street, one of Havre de Grace's two downtown business streets (the other is St. John Street). We were on our way to Laurrapin Grille, another place that seemed to be on everyone's must-try list. In contrast to the airy and bright Tidewater Grille, Laurrapin was dark and cozy and intimate. Even with two museums under our belts we were early into the lunch hour and so had no trouble getting a table. Laurrapin (pronounced LAIR-a-pin) is, according to owners Bruce and Sherife Clarke, an Appalachian adjective used to describe especially delicious poor-folks food. Their take on it involves dishes made using locally produced ingredients and then kicking it up and over the top. Colby went with a seafood wrap of shrimp and crab with bacon while I took an American Spicy Tuna Roll, which was deep fried and served with pickled ginger and pineapple mayo. We shared an order of pork-fat fries with jalapeno ketchup. By the time we were done, we were so far over the top we could see Pennsylvania.

Just as we returned to Washington Street, we got a call from Kathy. She had been caught in traffic out of D.C., but was now well on her way. We gave her directions for getting to the boat. Colby and I set out for the boat too, but were brought up short by the sight of a little bit of Paris, stuck on to the end of an otherwise basic American downtown building. Through its shop window we could see a tower of brightly colored macarons. No, not those chewy cookie things; those are macaroons, which are no more related to macarons than McNuggets are to coq au vin. A macaron is a cream-filled cookie sandwich. The cookie part is made with almond flour and the filling is made with . . . well, mostly magic, I think.

Les Petits Bisous (little kisses) the shop sign said. It might just as well have said Come In and Eat Yourself Silly, because that's what we did. But not before we chatted for a few minutes with owner Wanda Hall, who learned to make macarons when she was home-ported in Paris while working for an international aid organization. After ending up in Havre de Grace (her military husband was posted at Aberdeen Proving Ground), she decided the town needed a first-class macaron shop. Colby and I agreed and picked out a generous selection of flavors. We meant to save some for Kathy, but before we had reached Girard Street, we had eaten every one. Oh, dear!

Kathy, of course, arrived hungry. We handed her a protein bar from the galley cupboard and told her she'd have to wait. "Museum first," we said righteously, explaining that we'd already done two of them while we were waiting for her (leaving out the part about lunch and macarons). And so we set off for the Lock House Museum, all the way uptown.

This time we went up Market Street to St. John and then zigged up Water Street, all the while paralleling the shoreline. We zigged a final time at Conesteo Street, but not before we had to drag Kathy past Price's Seafood. "Museum first," we insisted. Later, we had to pull Kathy away again, but this time from the museum, where she insisted on asking the docent questions about this old-time bed warmer and that 19th-century potato masher. Meanwhile, Colby and I kept looking out the second-story windows at the river and the broad lawn once bisected by the Susquehanna and Tidewater Canal, which ran 45 miles from Havre de Grace to Wrightsville, Pa. The brief heyday of the canal system—mid to late 1800s—ended with the coming of the railroads. The Havre de Grace lockkeeper's house was considerably bigger than most because it housed not only the keeper and his family but the tax collection office as well.

*A quiet late-afternoon scene at Havre de Grace Marina at Log Pond,* Moment of Zen's *home base for the visit.*

The canal itself had been long ago covered over, except for some stone-work where this first (or last) lock in the system stood. I was fascinated with how the water, cut in to form the basin of present-day Havre de Grace Yacht Center, still flows from there to the old lock foundation.

Now it was Kathy who did the dragging. "Museum done, dinner now," she said simply, making a beeline for Price's Seafood. Colby and I followed dutifully behind, and we were soon studying the menu, deeply regretting that last half-dozen macarons. All around us we could hear the crack of crab mallets as dozens of steamed crabs were reduced to piles of broken shell. Price's is a Havre de Grace institution (it opened in 1943) and is still as popular as ever. Kathy made short work of her order of mussels and seafood gumbo, while Colby did a remarkable job on her crab imperial, rendered a little less grand by spectacularly overcooked green beans. I got so busy eating my seafood mac and cheese that I nearly forgot I was already full. Kathy reminded me and offered to finish it off. She's such a good friend.

Once back at the boat, we rallied enough to feed the dogs, and we all set out once more to give them a walk. "Let's get ice cream at Bomboy's," Kathy suggested. "But we've run out of museums," I protested. "No," she said, "there's a kind of tree museum in Tydings Park. I read somewhere that pretty much every tree there is a different type, and they're all labeled. That's worth at least a scoop of Rocky Road!"

So, of course, we stopped at Bomboy's, another Havre de Grace insti-

*A view of the Susquehanna River from Havre de Grace, looking upstream to the CSX railroad bridge and, beyond that, the U.S. Route 40 bridge.*

tution (founded in 1976), with Bomboy's Traditional Home Made Candy on one side of Market Street and Bomboy's Ice Cream on the other. A few minutes later, we could be seen strung out along Market Street, trying to walk the dogs and keep our ice cream from melting in the July air. I was a complete failure at the project and returned to the boat an hour later looking more like a two-year old learning to self-feed than the dignified adult I try so hard to be.

Footsore and full-bellied, we retired early. The next morning, over coffee, we discussed our situation. With no more museums to visit, could we justify yet another restaurant? Silly question. An hour later, we were first in line for MacGregor's Restaurant's Sunday Brunch. MacGregor's is located on St. John Street, just above and behind Tidewater Grill, so it too has a fine view of the water. My asparagus and crab quiche was delicious, as was Kathy's shrimp omelet and Colby's rockfish Benedict. Satisfied with a job well done, Kathy left soon after brunch to avoid the Sunday rush back to Washington. Colby and Lacey lingered only a little longer before they too headed south on I-95. Then it was time for Ivan and Jerry and everyone else I'd met that weekend at the marina to stop by to say good-bye as they headed for their respective homes. Skipper and I spent a quiet night on the boat, walking around town once more at dusk, and eating very little for dinner. Before going to bed, I started thinking about what other towns would work with my boat/museum/restaurant scheme. Surely there were quite a few, I thought, and then remembered I was still really full.

---

This article first appeared in *Chesapeake Bay Magazine* in December 2013. Jody Argo Schroath is senior editor of the magazine and editor of its annual *Guide to Cruising Chesapeake Bay*.

*Bohemia River:*

# 2

## Back To Bohemia

*Beauty without the beer and skittles.*

*by Jody Argo Schroath*

A great blue heron, wings fixed and head retracted, bisected the empty river, flying fast and low like a bass boat headed for a new hot spot. Unlike a bass boat, this efficient fishing machine was silent, utterly silent . . . like the Bohemia River over which it flew on this dreary spring day. Above the heron, a low ceiling of cloud spread dark and unbroken as far as the eye could see. The sky, the water, the vegetation—a landscape in monochrome. Only the suggestion of green at the tree tops betrayed the season. . . .

"Tell me again why we're here?" my friend Kathy asked as she emerged from the Albin 28's cabin, pulling on a powder blue fleece and shivering ostentatiously in the chill air. Reluctantly I tore myself away from the heron and the melancholy river to look at her.

"There are in fact two reasons that we're here," I said, "One reason is that it's late April, and I couldn't stand it any longer. I had to get out, even if the weather is still lousy."

"All right, I can understand that," Kathy said. "But why does getting out mean coming all the way up the Bay to the Bohemia River?"

"Ah, that's the second reason, which is a little more complicated," I replied, then paused to think about it for a minute before plunging ahead.

"You see, all of the other rivers I can think of in the Chesapeake were named for places back home in England—York and James, for example—or took the Indians' names—Potomac and Rappahannock, to name two—or were named for something about the geography or use—like Gunpowder and Back. All of them, that is, except the Bohemia, which is named for an ancient kingdom in central Europe."

"Where is Bohemia?"

"Where was Bohemia would be more accurate, since it's been defunct for nearly a century. Mostly in the Czech Republic," I said. "Prague was its capital. Good King Wenceslas of Christmas carol fame was one of its kings—a thousand years ago."

"I see," Kathy said. "We came four hours up the Bay from Annapolis on a cold gray day because this river was named for a country that doesn't exist. What was the river called before that?"

"The Oppoquermine River."

"Good choice."

"Oh, I suppose you'd just get used to saying it, like Pungateague and Piankatank," I said. "Still, to our ears Bohemia sounds rather romantic, don't you think?" She saw the treatise coming and sighed. "I know I'm going to regret this, but go ahead and tell me why this river got named Bohemia and, especially, why we're here."

Instead of answering right away, I turned my attention back to steering the boat. We had left Ford Landing at the north entrance to the Bohemia behind us, and I now eased the Albin slowly into Veazey Cove, to see how far in we could go before we ran out of water. With an eye on the depthsounder, I answered. "The reason we're here now is that the Bohemia in the summer is a crazy popular place. In another month or so, this place will be full to the brim with people having a good time—rafting-up, picnicking, water-skiing and swimming. It will be chockablock with kids and parents, aunts and uncles, friends and boats."

"And you're saying that's bad?"

"No, of course not." I pointed to where I had been watching the heron a few minutes earlier. "Look, here in Veazey Cove there are often a dozen or more boats rafted up. Added to that are the boats going to and from the C&D Canal, just around the corner. They pull in here for the night or to wait for the tide to change."

We had gotten about halfway into the broad cove, and the depth now dropped to four feet. I turned to run parallel to the cove's shore. "That's that," I said to myself, the question of how far being answered. I turned back to Kathy. "Obviously Veazey's not very good shelter against a north wind—or anything close to it," I said, "but there are other places upriver that will solve that problem. I'll show you in a little bit."

"That is all very useful information," Kathy said, "and on some level it's even interesting, but I still haven't detected a point. So far, I see that instead of lots of people we have no people. But why?"

She seemed to be getting a little testy, so I tried again. "I wanted to come here exactly because there would be nobody here. I wanted to see the Bohemia just once without the beer and skittles, without the kids and dogs and hot dogs—except Skipper, of course." I looked around, and then not seeing him asked, "Where is that dog?"

"Where he's been since we passed Love Point," Kathy replied, "asleep in the cabin, probably pulling the covers over his head."

"Oh," I said, as we edged past Battery Point at the eastern edge of Veazey Cove. Across the river were three of the river's more than half-dozen marinas: Two Rivers, Bohemia Vista Yacht Basin and Bohemia Bay Yacht Harbor. The Bohemia is only four miles long, but has more than its

*Skipper, the author's able-bodied seadog, stands watch on the bow.*
*Preceding page: The miniature lighthouse at Bohemia Bay Yacht Harbour on the river's north shore.*

share of marinas.

"And the reason I wanted to see the river without people in it," I said, pulling my train of thought back onto its track, "was that I wanted to see what Augustine Herrmann saw when he chose this spot because it looked like his native Bohemia." Herrmann (since orthography was not an exact science in the 17th century, the name is spelled variously Herrmann, Herrman and Herman) not only changed the river's name to Bohemia, but he named his property Bohemia Manor and he even added Bohemius to the end of his own name, just to be sure everyone knew he was from Bohemia. Herrmann had come to the Chesapeake by way of New Amsterdam when he was sent by Peter Stuyvesant to talk the Calverts out of enforcing their claim to the Delaware Bay by invading it. Once Herrmann had accomplished that, he decided he'd like to live here on the Oppoquermine and went to Lord Baltimore to ask for land in exchange for mapping the Chesapeake. Lord Baltimore complied, granting him tens of thousands of acres from the now Bohemia River into Delaware. He was also made a citizen of Maryland—its first naturalized citizen, in fact.

I took a deep breath and looked over to see whether Kathy had dozed off, since she hadn't interrupted my story. She seemed awake, so I blurted out what I'd really wanted to say all along: "And I wanted to see it that way because I've been to the original Bohemia, the former kingdom, without actually seeing it. Twice."

"I feel a long story coming on," Kathy said.

"I'll save it for dinner," I promised.

By this time we were well clear of Battery Point and headed for Long Point. Before we reached it, I turned the Albin sharply to port to take the river's first marker, flashing red "2", on our starboard. The channel narrows here and stays narrow until just beyond the 30-foot high Route 231 bridge, though the water outside the channel can be five to six feet deep. Beyond heavily riprapped Long Point, we spotted Long Point Marina, the first of the Bohemia's south-shore facilities. Soon after, we passed the entrance to Scotchman Creek and its low fixed bridge. Scotchman is a lovely creek, best explored with a kayak or dinghy, so I eased the throttle into neutral, and we coasted up to the empty outer dock at the marina there, called Aquamarina Hack's Point.

"Why are we stopping?" Kathy asked.

"So many questions!" I replied. "It's time for lunch. . . . Oh, nice to see you again, Skipper!"

"Hooray!" Kathy exclaimed happily and jumped down onto the dock. I snapped a leash on Skipper, and we trailed along after her rapidly retreating figure. "Where are we eating?" she asked over her shoulder.

"Hacks Point General Store. It's the only place to eat on the Bohemia River."

"You mean it's better than everything else?"

"No, it's the only place to eat."

"Oh."

"Just wait. You'll like it."

Kathy, Skipper and I trooped single file across the Glebe Road bridge over Scotchman Creek, past the entrance to Richmond Marina, just up the creek, then turned left as Glebe Road made a sharp turn at Ferry Point Road. Three moderately short blocks later, we walked into the parking lot of Hacks Point General Store.

Leaving Skipper attached to a picnic table, we went inside and ordered the special of the day, homemade chili, then took our order outside and rejoined Skipper. The chili was hot (both kinds of hot) and delicious and the ideal antidote to the day's chill. Hacks General Store offers the usual sundries, like dish soap and Little Debbie cakes, but it also has comfy chairs and a sofa coffee-bar style, with six varieties of horse magazines on the coffee table (horse farms are a big part of the northern Bay). Most important for our purpose, the general store features a popular deli with a wide range of sandwiches made on demand.

When we were done, we decided to walk over to Long Point Marina before going back to the boat. The neighborhood of Hacks Point, which is part of the town of Earleville, consists of modest cottages and neat small homes, many of them empty on this off-season midweek afternoon. At Long Point, we chatted briefly with the only person we found, hard at work on a power station at the end of one of the docks. Yes, he told us, the water at Long Point was only three feet deep in the slips, but it was a great place to keep a shallow-draft boat. He had kept his boat here for years, he said. Where did he boat? I asked. "We usually just motor straight across the river and drop anchor off the beach there," he said, pointing at the opposite shore. "It's a great place to swim and picnic, and there are always lots of people and kids there. That's the best thing." He added: "But if I go out of the river, it's usually to the [Susquehanna] Flats to go fishing."

We left Long Point and headed back to the boat, stopping along the way to take a quick look at Richmond's Marina before recrossing Glebe Road bridge. Less than a minute after pulling away from the Hacks Point dock, we were passing the marina and boatyard called Bohemia Anchorage, which is sandwiched between the Route 231 bridge and a stand of fine big trees. A good-looking facility, I noted, worth checking out next time through. We skirted the marina's dock, which reaches to the edge of the channel, and went under the bridge, choosing the marked passage through the far right span.

---

"We're on our own now," I said a few minutes later as we approached Georges Point, where the Bohemia splits in two—Little Bohemia Creek to the right and Great Bohemia Creek to the left. I don't know how they decided which was going to get which since they both seemed to be about the same size to me. Both also have narrow channels of deep water (six to nine feet), though the Great Bohemia's deep water reaches farther upstream. Neither creek's channel is marked however. We followed Little Bohemia first and immediately found ourselves idling down a lovely winding alleyway of trees and farmland. I quickly got cold feet, though; I had noticed earlier, out on the river, that the GPS on the chartplotter was consistently and significantly mislocating us, so I thought it would be pretty foolish to depend on it now to keep us to a channel that was only a few feet wide. And if we were to run aground, I felt pretty sure Kathy wouldn't be volunteering to walk out the kedging anchor. So we spun around and gave the Great Bohemia a try. It was, if anything, even more beautiful than the Little Bohemia. Here surely was a place unchanged by time. Trees along the creek blocked all but occasional tantalizing glimpses of the fields and fences, barns and great homes that lay beyond.

"Oh, I wish we had kayaks!" I said.

"We can only do so many things," Kathy countered.

Yes, I thought, we always think we have such crowded lives, but what about the Colonials? They all seemed to live a dozen different lives. Thomas Jefferson, to take an obvious example, was famously a statesman, intellect, architect, farmer and inventor . . . and that was just before breakfast. Even the nearly forgotten Herrmann is referred to in biographical sketches as an entrepreneur, merchant, diplomat, mariner, surveyor and cartographer. His map of the Chesapeake Bay is remarkable for its accuracy, with every river and stream in its place. And that was in 1670! In addition, according to some biographies, Herrmann had a road constructed from the upper part of the Bohemia—quite possibly exactly where we were at the moment—to Appoquinimink River (which he obviously didn't bother to rename), a tributary of the Delaware Bay. To get around an English embargo on foreign trade, ships loaded with tobacco would come up the Bohemia and then be hauled out and dragged on sledges by oxen the eight miles to the Appoquinimink, and thence sailed to Holland.

I came abruptly out of my reverie as I realized that the shallow water was quickly closing in on us and the oxen to pull us out were long gone. As beautiful as this was, it was time to go. So once again we spun carefully in our own length and left Great Bohemia Creek behind as well.

As we approached the bridge, I called Skipper—who had been pretending he was a hood ornament—back into the cockpit. Just before the bridge, we passed one of the river's favorite beaches along the north shore. With no more than a foot or two of water, it was definitely too shallow for us, but it did look inviting, even on a cold dark day. On the other side of the bridge, however, the water is deeper closer to the beach, and we idled in to within a few hundred feet. Then we followed the shoreline until we reached the place I'd been looking for all along, Manor Creek, my favorite place on the river. The mouth of Manor Creek is nearly hidden by a spit of land that leaves only a narrow passage open to the river. Before we had reached it, however, we caught sight of its namesake, Bohemia Manor. Herrmann's original home had overlooked the

*A view from Bohemia Bay Yacht Harbour, looking upstream to Hack Point and the Route 213 bridge.*

river just a few hundred yards from the current Bohemia Manor (c. 1920) that now slipped into view, with its elegant Georgian lines and broad lawn sloping down to the river. The house and the creek lie in a lovely little cove that is a nearly perfect anchorage, a fact not overlooked by summer boaters. But it was not sufficiently alluring to capture our fancy this time. We decided to continue our trip back down the river.

----

The afternoon was drawing to a close as we reached the first of the marinas on the north shore. I picked up the mike of the VHS radio and put in the call. "This is Bohemia Bay Yacht Haven," the reply came. A few minutes later, we turned into the marina's entranceway, marked by a little lighthouse, and nestled up against the marina's long fuel dock. Just as we finished making the lines fast and hooking up the shore power, the clouds that had been hanging over our head all day drifted away to the east, and the sun at last shone. It lit up the tree-lined shores and turned the new green leaves neon bright. The boats lying to their moorings, shone ochre against the suddenly blue sky.

We collected Skipper and walked and walked, going methodically up and down each dock, examining every boat, returning to the Albin just as the sun disappeared for good and the chill returned like an unwanted guest.

After we had closed ourselves into the Albin's cabin, I pulled out a pot

*A cabin cruiser anchored in the Bohemia River, under the gaze of historic Bohemia Manor.*

of Bohemian potato soup I had made for the occasion and set it on the stove to heat. (Okay, I called it Bohemian potato soup for effect; potato soup is pretty much potato soup, good though that is.) I sliced a loaf of good crusty bread, and we sat down to eat. As we ate, I told Kathy how I had visited Bohemia without seeing it. It was a romantic tale, which is to say it was lamebrained in the doing but heroic in the memory. Here it is:

In August 1968, I was aboard a student ship sailing from New York, bound for Le Havre, France. (A student ship, for those too young to remember, was a small oceanliner just this side of the scrap heap whose passengers were composed entirely of college students on their way to study in Europe or going back from studying in America.) During the eight-day passage, I became friends with a brother and sister who were returning to their native Czechoslovakia after a year in America.

While we were still at sea, news reached us that on August 21 the Soviet Union had invaded their country with troops and tanks, putting an end to the Czech's short-lived Prague Spring—the precursor of 1989's Velvet Revolution, which finally overthrew the Communist regime and ended Soviet domination. But the first attempt at freedom had ended badly, and the brother and sister were afraid they would be arrested at the border as Western sympathizers. So we, their new friends, decided that we would go with them, sneaking across the border from Austria to make sure they were safely picked up by relatives who were to meet them not far from the border to take them to Prague, where they lived.

Why we thought we would be more help than hindrance to them, I have no idea. But the brother and sister seemed happy enough to have the company, so we put the plan into action. We took a train to the nearest station to the Czech border, then walked along a back road for a while before leaving that to cross the border in the woods. When we were pretty sure we were over the border, we picked up the road again and walked on. Oddly enough, it worked. We waited just off the appointed intersection until the uncle's car arrived, hugged the brother and sister good-bye, and retraced our steps until we reached the railway station and disappeared into free Europe.

It was a distinctly idiotic idea, but it had the result of causing me to look over my shoulder for several years afterward, and of having a secret kinship with that country. Not that I saw anything—I was much too frightened and it was much too dark. I did finally get to Prague. It was a few years after the Velvet Revolution, and my husband, two daughters and I entered the new Czech Republic by car from Austria—in broad daylight this time—and headed for the capital city. I'd like to say I finally got to see Prague and its river, the Moldau, and the Bohemian countryside, but I got food poisoning from coffee I bought at a roadside stand only a few miles inside the border and spent the remainder of the visit suffering the consequences. I'm told it's indeed lovely.

---

Later that night, the wind picked up and ushered in a new set of clouds. About 1 a.m. I could feel the boat tugging hard against its stern line, so I got up and doubled the lines before tumbling back into the cabin and bed. Since Kathy had called dibs on the dog, I pulled on an extra sweatshirt against the cold and finally got warm just as dawn brightened the portholes. We made coffee, took a quick walk in the cold gray dawn, and we were soon ready to go. We collected our lines and returned to the river, heading west out of the river and toward the Elk. The wind was calm and the water utterly still. A light mist rose along the shore.

"You know, it's really quite beautiful, in an austere and colorless way,"

*Waterfront homes near Town Point, on the north side of the mouth of the Bohemia River.*

Kathy said. "Like a black and white photograph," I said. "Did you find what you were looking for?" she asked, settling herself in with a magazine. I thought for a minute and then answered: "Yes, I think I did. I still don't know for certain, of course, but—in my mind anyway—this is what I missed seeing all those years ago. Only there won't be any tanks waiting for us on Town Point. And this is why Herrmann picked out this place to call Bohemia." Then I added, "On the other hand, I'm now definitely ready for the summer Bohemia, with all the beer and skittles!"

At the mouth of the Bohemia, we looked up and down the Elk for shipping traffic, then I pushed the throttle forward and we turned left for home, leaving the Old Country behind.

---

This article first appeared in *Chesapeake Bay Magazine* in June 2011. Jody Argo Schroath is senior editor of the magazine and editor of its annual *Guide to Cruising Chesapeake Bay*.

*Middle River:*

# 3

## Destination Middle River?

*They keep all those boats there for a reason, you know!*

*by Jody Argo Schroath*

Really, what was I thinking? I was so anxious for
the boating season to begin this year that I took my
boat up to Middle River in mid-April. Mid-April!
You'd think I'd know better. But, no, I was eager
to explore the upper Bay and figured Middle
River would be the perfect stepping off place.
So I arranged for a slip for a month at Bowleys Marina.
That way, I thought, I would be able to come and go at my
leisure. Well, I did have a lot of leisure, as it turned out. But there
was very little coming and going, as I sat watching one spring storm after
another come rolling down from the north, roiling up the Bay and send-
ing down buckets of cold rain. Day upon day, Skipper the ship's dog and
I sat and watched it rain. Then we watched Fred and Ethel Mallard build
a nest inside the steps of our finger pier. Then we went for a long wet
walk, after which Skipper cadged dog treats from Mary McDonald in the
marina office. Still it rained.

It all came to a head two weeks later when my daughter Kristen and
her dog Echo came to visit and found Skip and me watching the weather
and investigating whether Ethel had laid her daily egg. "Enough!" Kristen
said. "Surely there's some place we can go." And she was right, of course,
because we had someplace to go right on our doorstep. So for the next

two weeks, we spent just about every minute that it wasn't storming—and more than a few that were—exploring Middle River. In fact, I got to know Middle River so well that now I'm ready to recommend it an excellent cruising destination!

"Cruising destination?" I hear you say, "I thought Middle River was the place you leave from rather than go to? After all, there's nothing there but a zillion boats and half as many marinas."

Well, yes, there are a lot of boats and marinas. In fact, I'd guess that per square foot of waterfront, Middle River has more boats and more marinas than anywhere else on the Chesapeake. But there's a good reason for that: It has a nearly perfect location. Middle River is tucked in beside Baltimore yet is also convenient to eastern Pennsylvania and New Jersey. It's also an easy cruise from there to any number of popular destinations, like Rock Hall, Annapolis, the Inner Harbor, Havre de Grace, Still Pond, Worton Creek . . . I could go on.

On the other hand, cruisers tend to overlook Middle River as a stop-over because it has about a zillion boats there already and it doesn't have a destination port of its own. Even the two zillion people who keep their boats on Middle River tend to take it for granted. Yes, they will tell you, there are some nice places to drop anchor for an afternoon or night and, yes, there are plenty of dockside restaurants, but usually we go to Rock Hall or St. Michaels, etc.

In the early days of the 20th century, Middle River was the destination for legions of city dwellers and workers from nearby factories, like Bethlehem Steel, who rented weekend cottages and kept their little runabouts and sailboats there. The story of Miss Barbara, a legend of sorts at Stansbury Yacht Basin is a good example. Miss Barbara kept her canoe for many years at Stansbury on Dark Head Creek. Every weekend in the summer, Miss Barbara would take the street car out from the city to Hawthorne Street, then swim across to Stansbury's. (In later years, when it became available, she would take the bus and then walk.) Then she would get in her canoe and paddle out onto the creek to spend the day, knitting and listening to the Orioles game on her transistor radio.

For Mary at Bowleys—my dog Skipper's favorite bookkeeper—the river was a destination too. Mary spent many of her childhood summers on Sue Creek. She got her first boat—an old wooden rowboat—when she was 11, she remembers. Her mother let her take it out, but attached a long line to it that stretched to shore, so she could keep an eye on her.

This did not prevent Mary from untying it and going off on her own, or intentionally capsizing it and then swimming underneath—to the acute dismay of her mother.

With Mary and Miss Barbara in mind, Kristen and I decided that we would treat Middle River the old-fashioned way, as our own backyard playground. We anchored on Frog Mortar Creek and let the dogs paddle around to their hearts' content. We docked for lunch and dinner at half-a-dozen different restaurants. We tied up at a county park and hiked to the Martin Aviation Museum. We poked around at least a dozen marinas. On one particularly fine day, we did have a ripping good sail outside the river on Hawk Cove . . . but then, as usual, a storm came along and we scurried back for cover. We read, we walked, we kept an eye on Fred and Ethel. But mostly we cruised up one creek after another. It would be fair to say that over the next two weeks we got to know Middle River pretty well. And the more we did, the better we liked it.

So then how can I describe Middle River to you? I could take you with me on a cruise up each of the river's nine creeks, but I don't think that's really practical. Instead I've given a very brief description of each of the creeks in sections following the main text of this story. But here in the

*An exhibit aircraft at the Martin Aviation Museum at the still active Martin State Airport. Preceding pages: Boats docked at Bowleys Marina.*

narrative I'm reluctantly confining myself to just a few places on two of Middle River's creeks, Frog Mortar and Dark Head. My apologies to the other creeks—especially Sue and Hopkins—and all the fascinating places and stories I'm leaving out. Perhaps these gaps will encourage you to plan a Middle River cruise for yourself . . . though I don't recommend you go in April.

---

Middle River lies between lovely little Seneca Creek on the north and straight-as-an-arrow Back River on the south. The three make up Baltimore's traditional summer vacation getaway area. Middle River is the largest and most comprehensively populated of the three. For that reason, its entrance can be a daunting place on a summer weekend, as boats converge from every direction, inside and out, as they skirt the bar off Booby Point on the south and Bowley Bar on the north. Inside, however, the going is much smoother, as the water stays deep nearly to the shoreline. Sue Creek strikes off immediately to port and then broad Galloway Creek appears to starboard. Ahead to the west are the river's other tributaries—Hogpen, Norman, Hopkins, Dark Head, Stansbury and Frog Mortar—as well as the main stem, which is indistinguishable from one of its tributaries. Each of these branches is deep enough for at least a quick trip inside and most are deep enough to reach their head. All except Hogpen and Stansbury also have public boating facilities. In fact, the shoreline of the entire river is a porcupine's back of docks, interspersed with a jigsaw puzzle of marina piers. I fancy you could almost tour the entire river by jumping from one boat to the next.

Interestingly, nearly all of these marinas are just as they started out (only bigger and more modern)—family owned and operated. Maryland Marina on Frog Mortar Creek, for example, is in its fourth and fifth generation of Miskiewiczes. The family founded the business in 1946 as the Maryland Marine Manufacturing Company, producing rowboats for Montgomery Ward and Sears until the 1960s, and Lightning class sailboats.

Speaking of the colorfully named Frog Mortar Creek, the anchorage there, which I already mentioned, is probably the most popular on the river, because here the woods come down to a sandy shore—a little misleading since this area is part of Martin State Airport. One of its main runways lies just beyond the anchorage; yellow buoys warn boats, especially those with tall rigs, to stay clear. While the airport is now used primarily by small commercial aircraft and the Maryland Air National Guard, it was once part of Glenn L. Martin Company, where many of the nation's most famous aircraft were designed, tested and produced— including bombers such as the B-10 and B26 Marauder, and flying boats such as the *China Clipper* and the SeaMaster.

Beyond the runway, Kristen and I would sometimes pull in for lunch at the long floating dock belonging to Sunset Cove restaurant, next to Maryland Marina. (Sunset Cove opened this spring, replacing the popular Wild Duck Cafe.) Or we'd fix our own sandwiches and dawdle up the creek, passing Conrad's Ruth Villa and Parkside Marina on the point just opposite the Martin runway. This spot puzzled us until we learned that is used for parties, weddings and corporate outings. Here's the story: The site was developed in the 1920s with small summer cottages, including one named Ruth Villa, before being purchased by the Conrad family. During the Depression, the vacation business fell off, so the Conrads tried chicken farming. That didn't really work out so well either, so the family decided to cook the chickens and open a restaurant. The business eventually evolved into the catering and party-site business that continues today.

Beyond Ruth Villa and Parkside Marina, Frog Mortar Creek bears right and ends after passing Edwards Boatyard and Chesapeake Yachting Center. A small shopping plaza with a Walmart, hardware store and a couple of restaurants lies a short walk beyond Chesapeake Yachting Center—I mention this because it's as close as you can get to shopping on Middle River.

Since I've chosen to describe Frog Mortar, it seems only right to mention Dark Head Creek as well, since the two book-end Martin airport, and Kristen and I usually explored both on the same outing. Beyond Wilson Point, where Frog Mortar and tiny Stansbury Creek go off to the right, the main channel strikes off into Dark Head Creek, ending in a sharp right at Martin Lagoon, a deep turning basin at the creek's end. It was along this route that seaplanes were towed out of Martin Airport for testing. Now the basin is used by water-skiers and fishermen. (As a completely unrelated side-note, the basin is bordered by Stansbury Manor Apartments, built by Martin in 1939. Richard Nixon lived in apartment 900-D while working with the company on a flying boat contract for the Navy.) The basin is also bordered by Wilson Point Park, which has a couple of boat ramps with a short dock. Kristen and I tied up here one day and walked to the Martin Aircraft Museum, located in one of the commercial aviation buildings at the airport. It's a fair hike, but a good occupation for a rainy spring day. The museum is small, but fascinating, with exhibits on Martin airport, one of the nation's oldest and home of the first commuter airline. A short ride away (the docents will give you a lift) are a dozen or so equally fascinating unrestored old aircraft, some manufactured by Martin.

Leaving Dark Head Creek after yet another visit, I would invariably look for Miss Barbara's canoe as we passed Stansbury Marina, though of course I would have been very much surprised to find it. That was the thing about Middle River, though. While it seemed so much about the present, with its fast boats and modern marinas, its roots are not so very deep below the surface. And in the end, it was Middle River's ghosts that made me feel at home.

Even Bowleys had its ghost. Mary the bookkeeper told me about her one rainy day as we sat in the marina office and she handed the ever-eager Skipper yet another Beggin' Strip. "Her name is Mrs. Quinn. People say they've seen her walking by upstairs," Mary said, pointing over her head. The marina office is in an old building, originally a home and then

*Maryland Marina's Sunset Cove Restaurant, complete with floating docks and even a bit of sandy beach.*

a duck-hunting club that may have included presidents Grover Cleveland and Benjamin Harrison among its guests. Now it's the office and home of marina manager Ed Harwood—who had been listening to Mary's story, and who shrugged when asked if he'd ever seen Mrs. Quinn himself.

It wasn't long after this conversation that the ghost of spring appeared at last and the weather turned perfect for cruising. But the calendar had turned too, and my time at Bowleys was up. Kristen and Echo packed up and headed back to Ohio, while Skipper and I undid our dock lines, said good-bye to Ed, Mary, Fred and Ethel, and headed out onto Middle River a final time. By the time we reached Hart-Miller Island, I had the sails set and the autopilot on. Skipper was sleeping under the cockpit table, Mrs. Quinn was walking the foredeck and Miss Barbara was seated in the stern, her knitting on her lap. We all had a great sail back to Annapolis.

## Frog Mortar Creek

Frog Mortar Creek heads north off Middle River for a mile and a half, sharing its entrance (Galloway Point to the east and Wilson Point to the west) with tiny Stansbury Creek. The main channel is 7 to 8 feet deep nearly to its head and 4 to 6 feet elsewhere nearly to the shoreline. Along its modest length, boaters can find just about anything they are look- ing for, with nearly half-a-dozen marinas, a very nice anchorage with trees and sand, a good dockside restaurant, access to modest shopping, a boatyard and a front-row seat for plane-watching. That's a lot to pack into a short, fully developed piece of real estate. But Frog Mortar is up to the job. Anchoring opportunities begin along the west side of the creek, soon after passing the entrance to Stansbury Creek—you may well find a boat or two already lying at anchor. Most powerboats back up nearly to the shore to take advantage of the better holding bottom there. In addition to marinas like Long Beach (just opposite the Martin State Airport run- way), Maryland and Tradewinds, you'll pass Parkside, part of Conrad's Ruth Villa, a catering and party facility. At the top of the creek, you'll find Edwards Boatyard and Chesapeake Yachting Center, a short walk from a Walmart and small strip mall.

## Galloway Creek

Broad Galloway Creek is located just beyond Bowley Bar at the mouth of Middle River. Since it is nearly as broad as it is deep it feels more like a bay than a creek. At its eastern edge lies Bowleys Marina, the river's largest, with about 1,000 slips. The marina is owned by its slipholders, and its slips are protected on the south and west by tall storm walls—a hard lesson learned after extensive damage from tropical storm Isabel. The best way to enter Galloway is to favor the Bowley side until clear of the Log Point shoal, which reaches out nearly to the center of the entrance. Once beyond that, however, the water remains generally 5 to 6 feet deep, but shallows to 3 and 4 up the creek's two prongs and even less close to shore. While Galloway is a pleasant place to drop anchor on a quiet weekday night in summer, it is too broad and too exposed, especially to wakes from Middle River's busy entrance, to make it a comfortable weekend retreat. A second marina, Galloway Creek Marina, is located inside on the northeast shore.

The creek is part of Bowleys Quarters, named for its 18th-century owner, Daniel Bowley, a sea captain and merchant. According to most accounts, though not all, Bowley kept his slaves on this peninsula, fenced in so they couldn't escape. A century later, the area became a game preserve, dotted with duck hunting clubs that attracted the rich and famous. In the 20th century, the area became a vacation spot for working-class Baltimore.

## Stansbury Creek
Stansbury Creek, tucked in behind Wilson Point at the entrance to larger Frog Mortar Creek, is short, sweet and very quiet. It carries 5 to 6 feet in the center most of its three-quarters of a mile length. If you venture in, beware of shoals that reach nearly to the center off opposing points about a quarter of a mile in. Stansbury is one of only two Middle River creeks (Hogpen is the other) that offer no marinas, though there is a private facility at the head of the creek. The eastern shore, part of Martin State Airport, is lovely and wooded, and the creek is well protected, but there really isn't room to drop anchor.

## Dark Head Creek
Dark Head Creek splits off from the main stem of Middle River at Clark Point and ends in man-made Martin Lagoon just half a mile later. Yet, that's enough room to pack in three marinas, a waterfront restaurant, two parks and a popular water-ski area. It also has a tiny tributary of its own opposite the basin, Cowpen Creek, and a tiny cove, Chestnut. The

creek's channel (which is also the main channel that begins at the mouth of Middle River) is 6 feet deep up to and including Martin Lagoon. Stansbury Yacht Basin, which has been in the Blazek family since 1960, sits at the creek entrance, while Chestnut Cove Marina (formerly Wagus Marina) lies just beyond at the entrance to the cove. On the other side of the creek is Windy Hill Marina. Not far beyond the cove is West Point Park, which has two boat ramps, a small dock, a fishing pier, a long waterfront walkway and picnic area. Everything is pretty well fenced off to exclude boaters, except the short dock at the side of the boat ramps. The water here is 4 to 5 feet, so it's possible to tie up for a short period. Martin Aviation Museum can be accessed by following Beech Drive to Wilson Point Road, left to the first entrance to the airport. The museum is in the building to the right inside. The walk is perhaps half a mile. The museum (*www.marylandaviationmuseum.org*) is open Wednesday through Saturday, 11 a.m. to 3 p.m. In addition to their small exhibit hall, the museum has a collection of about a dozen old aircraft, including a couple of F100s and a Martin 4-0-4 airliner. At Wilson Point Park, the creek makes a sharp turn to the right to form the quarter-mile-long and 8-feet deep Martin Lagoon. Here you're likely to find a water-ski boat and perhaps a small fishing skiff or two. On the right, are the Stansbury Manor Apartments, built by Martin to house company executives. Finally, opposite the lagoon is Kingston Point Park, which has no boating facilities.

*The long, long docks at Bowleys Marina, which presides over the mouth of the Middle River just inside Bowley Point.*

## Headwaters of Middle River

A mile and a half upriver from its entrance, Middle River narrows to the size of one of its tributaries. There, Wilson Point Junction Light acts as a kind of traffic cone as Stansbury and Frog Mortar creeks split from the main stem to the north while Norman and Hogpen creeks split to the south. Three-quarters of a mile later, Dark Head Creek carries the main channel up to Martin Airport, while the river—6 to 8 feet deep in the center—makes a jog first west then north before passing under busy Eastern Avenue. Meanwhile, a final tributary, Hopkins Creek, makes its exit at the second jog. All in all it's a short but busy river right up to the end. The water is deep, and the shores are lined with private piers and marinas. The first of these marinas is Cutter Marine Yacht Basin, which has 125 slips, a pool and full service. Like many of Middle River's marinas, they are also boat dealers and brokers. Just beyond Cutter is another full-service family marina, Riley's. Some boaters like to anchor off the wooded section of the southern bank, not far beyond the entrance and before Cutter Marine. The water is deep and the spot is well protected— too protected perhaps for a hot summer night.

*A small privately built "lighthouse" marking one of the tributaries of Hopkins Creek.*

## Hopkins Creek

Hopkins Creek wins the contest for most facilities packed into a short run of water. And on Middle River, where you can't throw a muskrat without hitting a marina, that's saying something. And yet, it's one of the most charming places on the river, as well. It even has room for a nice anchorage. Hopkins splits from the main stem of the river not far beyond Clark Point and maintains 5 to 8 feet during its short run. On entering Hopkins Creek, you'll immediately spot the red roof of River Watch Restaurant and Marina, where you'll find very good food and lively entertainment on the weekends. The slips are in good shape and easy to access. Next door to River Watch is Middle River Yacht Club, which sits along the entrance to a small branch of the creek that curves around behind it. In this attractive backwater, you'll find the venerable Deckleman's Boat Yard. On the other end of this little branch is Essex Marina & Boat Sales, with lovely grounds and full service. The point where the little branch splits from the creek, is marked by a good-size private lighthouse. The anchorage? The shore opposite River Watch makes a good place for a boat or two to drop anchor. The longer branch of Hopkins is marked by the long docks of private Hopewell Pointe Marina, which parallel much of the shoreline.

## Norman Creek

Norman Creek leaves the main stem just northwest of Wilson Point Junction Light. Its run is short but it maintains 4 to 6 feet for its length. It even has a daymark, red "2", which should be carefully honored because it marks a shoal off Barren Point. Just inside lie tiny Norman Creek Marina to the right and Crescent Yacht Club, a boat and social club, to the left. The creek's largest facility, Sunset Harbor Marina, is located at its head. Like many of the marinas on Middle River, it is family owned and offers full service and all the amenities. If 4-foot depths work for your boat, exploring Norman Creek's many little coves will make a very pleasant way to while away a few quiet hours. Depths in the main channel run generally 5 to 7 feet.

## Hogpen Creek

Hogpen Creek shares the distinction with Stansbury Creek of being the only two Middle River tributaries that have no public boating facilities—

that is, no marinas and no restaurants. That doesn't mean it's not worth a quick tour. Quick is the operative word, since Hogpen Creek is small, even by Middle River standards. It is also uncharacteristically shallow. You'll find a short finger of 6 to 7 feet at the entrance, which promptly ends as the water shallows to 2 to 3 feet for the remainder. Local knowledge may very well get you more, though, since the creek is lined with docks and boats. My timid explorations were decidedly of the shallow variety however, so barring the acquaintance of a resident, a trip by dinghy would be the safest bet.

## Sue Creek

In a contest for prettiest creek on Middle River, Sue Creek would be my choice, despite the fact that its unmarked waters beyond the entrance make for nervous cruising. The depths are charted at 4 to 5 feet, but in my tours I usually managed to find the bottom at least a couple of times, though happily only just. Sue Creek is the first tributary off the main stem, splitting off to the southwest at Sue Island, not far beyond Booby Point. The large flagpole and clubhouse of the Baltimore Yacht Club make foolproof landmarks. It is essential not to make a beeline for the

*A typical Middle River cottage not far from the upper river's main stem, this one with a pier built for multiple boats.*

entrance mark, though, because the water is shoal off the length of Sue Island. Then be careful to obey the mark at the entrance—flashing green "1"—because the water is also shoal off Turkey Point to the north. In fact, most boats hug the marker pretty tightly. This leaves you facing the yacht club's fuel docks, which makes a convenient stop, although there's fuel aplenty on the river. The yacht club's restaurant is open to the public, a happy circumstance because the food is very good. The water remains deep just off the docks, but from there on you are on your own. It's worth the trip, though, because there are anchorages, sandy beaches and plenty of trees. Sue Haven Yacht Club is located in a branch running north, while Red Eye Yacht Club is farther up the main creek. In a cove behind Baltimore Yacht Club, you'll find Holly Neck Marina and Sue Island Yacht Basin. Sue Island, by the way, has long been attached to the mainland by a causeway.

This article first appeared in *Chesapeake Bay Magazine* in September 2012. Jody Argo Schroath is senior editor of the magazine and editor of its annual *Guide to Cruising Chesapeake Bay*.

*Sassafras River:*

# 4

## Wait For It . . .

*The best recipe for a perfect fall cruise on the Sassafras River? One part patience and one part good company.*

*by Jody Argo Schroath*

This story is about three things—the lovely Sassafras River, the singular pleasure of cruising in the fall and . . . well, waiting. Fall is a terrific time for a cruise, the perfect time to just look around, to admire the glorious show of turning leaves without the bustle and sociability of summer. My friend Kathy and I had decided that we would cruise up "north" to the Sassafras, simply to see the river and admire its beauty before everything went bare and winter set in. We didn't even care if we talked to a soul. We were just going to cruise. "That's what fall cruising is all about," we told ourselves as we waited for just the right moment to set out. "That and eating," Kathy added. "It's always about eating," I replied.

Waiting for just the right moment isn't easy in the best of times, but it's even worse when the waiting stretches into weeks and weeks, which naturally is what happened last year as we monitored a variety of internet leaf-watching sites and waited for fall, with its flash-in-the-pan finery, to drift down from the north to the Atlantic seaboard. Finally, the "peak" began to creep down out of Quebec into New England and then shot an arm down the Allegheny Mountains. It was time to start calling friends and casual acquaintances who lived in Kent and Cecil counties—the two counties that border the Sassafras River. "Any color yet?" I'd ask. "Not yet," they would reply. "Now?" I'd ask the following week. "No," came the unvarying reply. Meanwhile, the days grew shorter and the nights grew colder. Finally, the last week in October, the answer came back, "Now!"

Hooray, the wait was over! I alerted Kathy and canceled all my plans (those Kardashians would just have to wait). A few days later, the dock cart was piled high with bedding, charts, fleece vests and dog food, and the three of us—Kathy and me and my dog Skipper—were headed down the dock to the Albin 28 *Journey*. Half an hour later we pulled out of J Port Annapolis and into Back Creek. The air was sweet and clear. Annapolis harbor was silent in the morning chill as *Journey* plowed silver furrows in the still blue water. A few minutes later, we rounded the marker off Greenbury Point, turned north toward the center span of the Chesapeake Bay Bridge and settled in for the ride. Skipper curled up in his bed in front of the passenger seat and Kathy fell sound asleep over a book in the V-berth. Well, I was enjoying the scenery, anyway.

Hugging the eastern shore, *Journey* had soon passed Love Point at the mouth of the Chester River and then Swan Point and Rock Hall. We were just opposite Worton Creek when Kathy emerged from below wearing a bright pink fleece pullover and carrying a bag of salt and vinegar potato chips. She climbed over the still-napping Skipper to get into the passenger seat. "Mmm," she said by way of a conversation opener. "Almost there," I replied, knowing she was probably still too sleepy to take in a detailed geographical description. Skipper was awake now too and making a cottage industry out of picking up dropped potato chips.

"Don't eat too many chips," I said, sounding just like somebody's mother, "you'll spoil your lunch . . . and it's a humdinger, I promise."

"You have nothing to worry about, I'm always hungry," Kathy replied.

We passed Worton Creek and then Still Pond. As we drew closer to the Sassafras I imagined us climbing steadily north, like the New Yorkers who stream out of the city and up into Vermont's Northern Kingdom each fall to be dazzled by the countless sugar maples and their iridescent reds and burnt oranges. In fact, as we got farther north, we did see more and more color in the trees along the banks. At Howell Point, which marks the southern entrance to the Sassafras, we turned east to begin our trek upriver, passing a particularly vivid stand of that peak color we'd waited for so patiently.

Three miles or so later we were opposite Grove Point, the northern shore of the mouth of the Sassafras. The river's significant "underbite" has a distinct affect on the life of the river; it creates a kind of colossal funnel for the debris that comes bobbing down the Bay from the Susquehanna River. This means that whenever the flood gates of the Conowingo Dam are thrown open after particularly large rains or snow melts, the protruding lower "jaw" of the Sassafras catches a great deal of the debris—dead trees, old kitchen appliances, etc.—that comes along with the floodwater.

The same geography also leaves the town of Betterton, only two miles upriver from Howell Point, exposed to ship wakes and winter northerlies. On this lovely fall day, however, there were neither northerlies nor Frigidaires to contend with so we made our first Sassafras landing at Betterton's municipal pier. It's a fine pier, with plenty of water, and on this off-season day it was entirely empty. As was Betterton's beach. The Betterton beach is a lot like a Florida beach—long and wide—but without the requisite line of hotels and condos. Oh, there are a few condos in Betterton to be sure, but most of them are tucked away and across the street. In Betterton's heyday as a resort destination, from the end of the 19th century until about halfway into the 20th, its hotels and cottages catered to thousands of vacationers who arrived by steamboat from

*Crab pots ready for deployment on the deck of a workboat at the wharf at Turner Creek County Park. Preceding pages: A set of stairs built into the river's frequently steep banks.*

Baltimore and points north. But the hotels and the tourists have been gone a long time, and Betterton has lain fallow, waiting for the fun to begin again. Or maybe not. Maybe the town's 370 residents prefer it this way. I rather think I might. Despite the current lack of amenities like restaurants and hotels, the beach attracts hundreds of fun-seekers all summer long. But we had it to ourselves for the moment and we made the best of it, strolling up and down the beach, the boardwalk and the streets, and then searching fruitlessly amidst the beachside vegetation for an old freshwater well I'd read about somewhere in some book or other . . . or at least I *think* it was at Betterton.

Back on the boat we went off in search of autumny things like, um, pretty leaves and stuff, and . . . well we'd know autumny when we saw it. About this time, I noticed that the potato chip supply was running dangerously low, so I suggested that we head for one of my top 10 favorite spots anywhere on the Bay—Turner Creek. There we'd be able to virtually wallow in fall, I explained to Kathy, who was now tipping the remains in the bag directly into her mouth as Skipper watched intently from below. And we could stop for lunch. "You'll love it," I said. "We can start with a crab bisque I made. It's super rich and has just a little sherry." I started to continue my recitation of the luncheon menu, but then noticed that we were just about to pass Lloyd Creek. "Wait, let's see if we can get into Lloyd Creek first. It's the new uber-popular summer party place on the river," I explained. "We should be able to make it into the creek, and the entrance is fun because it's almost impossible to see."

"Crab bisque? I love crab bisque!" Kathy said, then shrugged. "Well, okay, as long as it's right on the way."

The party moved to Lloyd Creek a few years ago, after the Sassafras's longtime favorite boat beach, Ordinary Point (just upriver and on the opposite shore), was riprapped along its entire length. Lloyd Creek has a long beach, perfect for beaching boats and picnicking—though boats that draw more than a couple of feet need to use a dinghy to get to the beach. The creek entrance, located at the extreme eastern end of a long spit of land, is so well hidden that even the redoubtable John Smith would have been hard put to find it—though, of course, who's to say he didn't?

Captain Smith did sail up the Sassafras River—which he named the Tockwogh, after the tribe of Indians he found here. Smith and his men got themselves invited to dinner at a tribal village, very likely located on Turner Creek, which Smith described as having a palisades around it, presumably for protection from the more bellicose Massawomecks. I don't know this for sure, but I imagine Smith liked the Sassafras. Who wouldn't? The river is deep for most of its 20-mile length, with a wide central channel—15 to 50 feet deep as far as the large natural harbor just below where Maryland Route 213 now crosses it, and six or seven feet out of the channel, nearly up to the riverbanks. On each side, lovely high bluffs, thick with maples, oaks and ashes, share space with farmland and handsome homes.

As we motored slowly toward the entrance to Lloyd Creek, those stands of hardwoods were luminous in shades of red, yellow and ochre in the midday sun. Soon we were so close to the shore that we were nearly in the shade of an old tulip tree. Just then, Kathy spotted the narrow passage. "That's it?" she asked. We edged through tentatively, like uninvited guests at a dinner party, but found no one at home. As Kathy marveled at the beach (as you might have already guessed, the Sassafras has some of the sweetest and most accessible beaches on the Bay), I kept an eye on the depth sounder. Six . . . five . . . four.

"I'm sure there's a channel here *somewhere*, I just don't know where," I said, trying several routes, all unsuccessfully shallow. Every time I'd been here before, I had been on other people's boats—boats with considerably shallower draft. "Well, you get the idea," I said finally, spinning the boat around and heading for the exit. "In the summer, this is just a conga line of boats backed up to the beach, having some fun."

As we turned back upriver, I continued to extol the virtues of the Sassafras. "In addition to great beaches and deep water, it has anchorages galore," I said, "and enough creeks to keep a gunkholer occupied for years."

"Can we gunkhole for some lunch now?"

"Sure. I made chicken salad with tarragon and roasted hazelnuts too. And I've got some lovely local Bibb lettuce to put it on! Turner Creek is just a little . . ." I interrupted myself, "Wait, before we do that, let me show you Ordinary Point, that *former* favorite beach I was telling you about. There, you can see the tip of it now coming in from the left." And before Kathy could object, I aimed for the opposite shore in the direction of a long finger of land that reached nearly to midstream. This was Ordinary Point, and it was indeed as neatly encased in white riprap as a finger in a Band-Aid—and presumably with the same end in view: protection from the elements. Kathy dutifully studied the shoreline and then looked wistfully back over her shoulder toward the entrance to Turner Creek. "So near and yet so far," she said under her breath.

But now I'd had another thought. "As long as we're on this side of the river," I said, "we might as well take a look behind Knight Island. It's a great anchoring spot, and I'll bet it's beautiful this time of year. After all, that's why we're here, right?" I didn't wait for her answer. "That's also near the dinghy landing for Mount Harmon, which is this splendid 1730 manor house with wonderful gardens and lots of trails. We could walk around for just a little bit anyway. Mmm, no, it's closed today. . . . Too bad, but we can come back another time."

"Not unless you feed me first."

A little over a mile upriver from Ordinary Point we turned up Back Creek and followed it around the tip of Knight Island, which is actually a peninsula. There we stopped in the dead-calm water of Back Creek and looked up into its tributaries, Carr and Foreman creeks, and the photostill reflection of the fall colors mirrored in them. Yes, it was absolutely beautiful. Exactly what we'd come to find on our fall cruise.

Kathy had no problem breaking the spell. "What else did you bring for lunch?" she asked as we returned to the main channel of the Sassafras.

*Workboats at Turners Creek at day's end. The well-protected creek and wharf is a favorite spot for watermen and recreational boaters alike.*

"At least I can *imagine* I'm eating it."

"Asparagus," I replied, heading upriver again. "Poached . . . white. Lightly poached and then chilled. I thought we'd just do a little lemon and olive oil and throw on some capers. It should be quite nice." She groaned quite audibly. Skipper looked up, worried.

"Just a little bit longer," I said. "I want to take you up to the bridge first. We're almost there and that's where all the marinas are." (I decided not to mention that's where all the restaurants are too.) One of the many great things about the Sassafras is that all of its marinas and restaurants are clustered together (with one exception) around the harbor just below the Route 213 bascule bridge. The result, from a practical standpoint, is that no matter which of the marinas you choose—and they are all great and all have transient slips—you'll find everything else, including all the restaurants (which are terrific), fuel docks, ship's stores and repair facilities, within easy reach. In addition, other essential businesses like a grocery store, pharmacy and package store can be found about a mile south on Route 213 in pretty little Galena (population 428). And because this is fresh water, it attracts a lot of classic wooden boats, which are always worth seeing, no matter what the season. The exception to the marina rule is Gregg Neck Marina, a fine old-fashioned boatyard, which lies on the other side of the bridge.

About two miles above Back Creek, with the bridge in sight, I slowed *Journey* to six knots. We passed Island Creek on the right, which has little Daffodil Island at its center—a further diversion, but one which I just managed to resist. Instead I pressed on toward the marinas and the bridge. Enough was enough, I thought. I was teetering on the brink of mutiny as it was. So a little while later I pointed out the entrance to Skipjack Cove Marina, the newest of the half-dozen marinas that have sprung up here over the past century. I had made my first trip on the Sassafras out of Skipjack Cove Marina, I explained, aboard a classic Chris Craft Roamer that lives there. Next, I pointed out Duffy Creek Marina, tucked into its private cove, and then the Granary Marina. "It's built on the site of an old granary—duh—which burned and was rebuilt as a terrific restaurant." Restaurant! Oops! I raced on: "The Granary is owned by the same family as Georgetown Yacht Basin, which is over there on the southern side and is one of the river's oldest. And there's Sassafras Harbor Marina, nearest the bridge on the north side." Sassafras Harbor started out as the Sassafras Boat Company and is the other oldest marina here, I explained. (What I didn't say was that they also have a nice little restaurant, called Harbor Cafe.) In between Sassafras Harbor and the Granary is Sailing Associates, whose great old trees and park-like setting make it look more like a yacht club than the marina it is. (And there, I thought to myself as I looked up at the fine old house perched on the south side of the bridge, is the Kitty Knight House, the queen of Sassafras restaurants. And I also didn't mention Skipjack Cove's restaurant, Signals. Or Twinny's Place, which is a crazy popular little place with great crab-cake, chicken and rockfish sandwiches, just down the road on the way to Galena.)

"Yipes, look at the time!" I exclaimed. "It's nearly four o'clock already. We'll just go through the bridge and up as far as Gregg Neck before we turn around. It's really pretty up there, and it will only take a couple of minutes."

Both Kathy and Skipper gave me a pretty bitter look as we waited for the bridge, but, really, it only added a few more minutes to idle past Mill Creek and then Gregg Neck Boatyard. "Look, there are some great boats there!" I said pointing toward the marina. As we reached Wilson Point, I could see by the chart that we were running out of room, and I was definitely running out of time. We glided to a stop, took in the narrowing river ahead of us, the marsh plants turning brown and curling in preparation for winter, and then turned around and headed back downriver, back to Turner Creek and the lunch that had now become dinner.

Turner Creek has a wide entrance that funnels down into a very narrow channel that nearly grazes the western bank along the way. It's a somewhat notorious channel, with stiff grounding penalties for those who stray. But it's also well marked and, if carefully followed, presents no problem. Inside, the creek widens into a small bay, with Turner's Creek Park approximately at its center. To the right the bay is shallow and wisely avoided, though it's deep enough for most boats from the last marker to the park, with its three-sided bulkhead, its pre-Civil War granary and pier. To the left of the park is a small anchorage, with several permanently anchored boats, but usually room for a few more. The park's picnic grounds lie on a bluff above the pier and offer a storybook view down to the little bay, to the circuitous entrance into the creek, to the Sassafras beyond and finally to the bluffs of the river's opposite shore. Looking down on all that through the trees on that bluff is, to me, one of the Chesapeake's loveliest sights.

During crabbing season, the bulkhead and pier are often busy with workboats and watermen unloading the day's catch. But as we sidled up to the pier in the deep yellow light of this fall afternoon, there wasn't a deadrise in sight. Like the rest of the river, we had the pier and the park to ourselves. Skipper was the first ashore. He and I had made this stop many times before, so he knew all the right bushes and all the best smells. Kathy and I transferred the containers with "lunch" into a picnic basket and walked down the pier and then climbed up to the picnic area above. In the waning afternoon light I poured out the crab bisque, while Kathy set out the lettuce on two plates and spooned mounds of chicken salad on top. I dressed the asparagus and pulled the cork on a bottle of Ingleside Winery's Chesapeake Chardonnay I had recently brought back from the Northern Neck. Then I set out a dish of Newman's dog kibbles and a big bowl of water for Skipper. We three ate avidly and silently, two of us looking out at the scene below us, admiring the colors of those perfectly peak autumn leaves. When we had eaten our fill, and then some, we packed up the remains and toted it all back to the boat. Then we pushed off from the dock and idled out into the little bay, dropped the anchor, and settled ourselves in the cockpit, watching the stars come out as the evening chill settled down around us.

"Good?" I asked.

"It pains me to say it," Kathy replied, "but you're right. That was worth waiting for . . . all of it." Then, after a pause: "What's for dessert?"

"Pear and cranberry crisp with a little vanilla ice cream," I said.

"Good, that will make a fine breakfast."

---

This article first appeared in *Chesapeake Bay Magazine* in October 2010. Jody Argo Schroath is senior editor of the magazine and editor of the annual *Guide to Cruising Chesapeake Bay.*

*Patapsco River:*

# 5

## Playground on the Patapsco

*Bright lights, Big City? Yeah, maybe, but Baltimore's Inner Harbor is also a big shoreside playground— ask any kid who's been there.*

*by Wendy Mitman Clarke*

The first time my family sailed to Baltimore, it was so hot the weathermen were predicting certain incineration for anyone foolish enough to spend time outdoors, followed by thunderstorms that would rock the world. They were right, but who cared? We had a blast. At the end of a long, sweaty, rollicking day of exploring the Inner Harbor and its myriad attractions by foot and water taxi, our son Kaeo bestowed on us what has to be the highest praise a child can give to his own parents: "I had so much fun today," he said, "I forgot you were grown-ups."

Last summer we set out to one-up that trip. I wanted to have so much fun that I would forget that I was a grown-up. We wanted to explore Baltimore's waterfront from a kid's point of view, find the best possible rides, find out how much fun we could pack into a three-day weekend before we all dropped—and since the kids are obviously more knowledgeable than the adults in this department, they got to determine most of the itinerary.

Fortunately for us, our kids (Kaeo is 7 and his sister Kailani is 4) love nothing more than going everyplace they can by boat, so the means of transportation was never in dispute. We would sail there. Of course. So off we set on a cool early autumn Saturday afternoon from Annapolis, riding a pleasant southerly under the Chesapeake Bay Bridge, past Sandy Point and Baltimore lights and up to the Patapsco River, where the first great ride of Baltimore begins—on the river itself. Just off the mouth, two dredges were carving out the channel, flanked by a pair of enormous barges and a couple of tugs scurrying about tending to things, as tugs do. The dredges' hinged buckets resembled the maws of enormous hippos, open as they plummeted to the bottom, then clamped shut when they broke the water's surface on the way up, mud and water sluicing from their gums.

"Wow!" Kaeo yelled, as the chutes and ladders and erector sets of the Bethlehem Steel plant at Sparrows Point hove into view. "That looks like a giant playground!" Sure, everything was grit and smoke, with black and blood-red buildings poking between the mountains of aggregate here and there, but if you put your kid glasses on, of course it's like a giant playground. Big orange cranes hunched like gigantic praying mantises, and just beyond, past the Key Bridge, the even taller, ganglier cranes of the Seagirt Marine Terminal poked up like the distant antennae of some inquisitive bug.

From the get-go, the Patapsco is all big, broad-shouldered and busy. I never get tired of coming here and just watching all the focused commotion of a hardworking river. Sailboats flit here and there, and now and then a go-fast boat or motoryacht will rumble by, but the river's true nature is in its muscle and its pure, unadulterated bigness. Diminished as they may be from Bethlehem Steel's heyday, the smokestacks and industry of Sparrows Point still dominate the river's northern skyline at the mouth, while more stacks, fuel terminals and tanks pop up on the southern shore like giant mushrooms. In between, the unexpectedly graceful span of the Key Bridge arches across the water. Though it's true that I love the solace of the Bay's quieter, more undisturbed places, there is something about this river—the ships, the tugs, the constant movement—that fills me with energy and excitement every time I visit.

As we reached under the bridge in the long, flat water, a pilot boat hustled past on its way to a ship we couldn't even see yet. Past abandoned Fort Carroll, whose gun ports eyed us with spooky, hooded darkness ("I'll bet there are skeletons in there," was Kaeo's deliciously grim historical assessment), we came upon Seagirt Marine Terminal, where bright containers were stacked alongside the long-legged blue cranes, and a small parking lot of new John Deere tractors (the trademark green and yellow gave them away) awaited shipping. To port, the new Vane Brothers (a tug, fueling and maintenance company) complex sprung up in Fairfield, its architecture artfully mingling a modern, airy design of arches and windows with something more reminiscent of the port's warehouses of the past. Ahead, the green sward of Fort McHenry was the only green in sight, really, in the hard-edged harbor.

Directly across from the fort we scooted past the *Atlantic Trader*, a huge black cargo ship that seemed close enough to touch, tied up at the cement terminal. With a procession of dump trucks alongside, the ship's cranes were executing a slow, methodical ballet of up, out, down, dump, up, in, down. . . . How long would it take to unload the whole ship like this, bucket by bucket?

Drawing closer to the Inner Harbor, we watched industry give way to recreation. Now, instead of huge ships and cranes lining the waterfront, there were recreational marinas, water taxis, the tour ship *Clipper City*—and sailboats tacking back and forth as powerboats cruised past. Float-

*One of the best views of Baltimore's Inner Harbor, from Federal Hill on the harbor's south side. Preceding pages: The National Aquarium as seen from Federal Hill.*

ing over the whole scene was a huge balloon on a long tether. "Wow, do you think we can go on that?" Kailani asked. "Don't see why not," I said, immediately regretting it. Was I completely insane? Me, with my kids up in that balloon with nothing but a skinny little cable connecting us to mother earth? I quickly added "We'll see," but to little effect. That horse was out of the barn.

The tugboat *Cape Romain*, heading out of its berth at Fells Point, tooted its whistle at the kids as they waved. And, getting one last glimpse of the maritime industry that founded this city, we slipped past the *Antilles* I tied up at the Domino Sugar plant, delivering its sweet-smelling cargo. Just beyond were the tall pilings and floating piers of HarborView Marina, our home for the weekend. The first great ride in the city—the ride up the river—was over.

---

The kids had a major weekend planned and a lot of ground to cover. First and foremost—since it was closest, and because we'd been there many times before—was the Maryland Science Center, specifically, its IMAX theater. We had barely gotten the lines on the dock before they were clamoring to head over there—it's a 15-minute walk from HarborView— and since one of the weekend's M.O.s was to avoid, as much as was reasonable, the dreaded "no" word, we said, sure, let's go.

The IMAX theater is simply amazing. Where else but in the real thing is the feeling of flying through the chicanes in a Formula 1 car so intense you find yourself leaning sideways out of your seat? Where else but at a shuttle launch can you feel the roar and fury of a rocket's struggle to overwhelm gravity in every bone and tissue in your body? Since an IMAX film can be such an intense experience, I was a bit concerned about my young daughter, but we started the evening with a big bucket of popcorn and an enchanting, gentle film called *The Living Sea*. It transported us from Baltimore to the Pacific islands of Palau, one of the seven "Underwater Wonders of the World." There we met a fairly isolated culture of people whose lives and livelihoods are entwined with the sea, and who respect and revere the ocean and their profound relationship with it. We immersed ourselves in the gelatinous world of Jellyfish Lake in Palau, we screamed down Hawaiian waves on the backs of surfers' boards, we barreled through the vicious surf at the U.S. Coast Guard Motor Lifeboat School at Cape Disappointment, Wash., we dove 3,000 feet under the sea in a remotely operated sub and came face to face with critters more alien than Venusians, we swam alongside humpback whales and listened to their haunting songs.

From there, it was off to the International Space Station in what is the first three-dimensional IMAX film, Space Station 3D. So real is the 3D imagery that when an astronaut tossed an orange and it floated gently, weightlessly toward us, we found ourselves leaning far out of our seats and holding out our hands to catch it. (I looked around and most of the audience was doing the same thing, and laughing in astonishment). Fortunately, Kailani had conked out in my lap by the time a Russian rocket blasted off to travel to the station. The liftoff was so powerful, dirt and gravel slammed into our faces and our bodies shook with the force of it. Then, just as suddenly, we were deep in the silent darkness of space, looking back at earth, at Palau, at Baltimore. When it was all over, we carried both kids back to the boat, where Kaeo fell asleep mumbling about becoming an astronaut.

———————————

Next morning it was off to Port Discovery, the "Kid-Powered Museum." We tried to take a water taxi from the stop at HarborView, but it seemed to be going everywhere but the aquarium, which was the closest stop to Port Discovery. So we opted for a land taxi instead—nowhere near as fun, but this time, at least, far quicker and more efficient. Port Discovery sits about a block up from the waterfront, with a clear view from its front door to the Coast Guard cutter *Taney* and the huge black stacks of the Power Plant (once an actual power plant and now a trendy mixed-use complex with restaurants, bars, office space and a vast Barnes & Noble bookstore). In front of Port Discovery is a brick courtyard a few blocks square which includes a fountain, an open cafe under some umbrellas, some trendy clubs with names like "Babalu" and "Mundo," and two life-size plastic giraffes that seem to be nibbling the urban foliage. Oddly, they don't seem out of place.

The museum's entrance clues you into its overriding sense of play; a huge glass arch with a peaked roof is framed by whimsical vertical sculptures covering two columns of corrugated metal, including a nice variety of propellers, metal grates squiggled around like rusty lace and some industrial light fixtures. This—plus the giraffes, little gardens of ornamental grasses and pansies, and the fountain complete with some smallish gargoyles—

results in a fun sort of sensory overload. Which seems to be the point.

Kailani was the first one to spot the balloon we had seen from the harbor, around the corner and clamped firmly to land at the moment. This was the HiFlyer, a huge helium balloon with an enclosed gondola for up to 30 passengers. The HiFlyer, I read from the museum's literature, is tethered by a steel cable. Upon liftoff, you are raised to a height of 450 feet, from which you can see God, or at least the entire harbor and maybe even the Eastern Shore on a clear day. On this crystalline autumn day, the wind was blowing about 20 from the northwest, and I had a perfectly clear vision of me and the kids in the gondola (there isn't much Johnny won't do, but heights top his "no way" list), the HiFlyer whipping in the breeze, the kids oohing and aahing and I trying in vain not to lose breakfast. "Can we go, can we go?" my daughter begged. Divine intervention, that's what I needed—either that or a handy aunt or uncle. I got the former, or so it seemed, when the person at the ticket counter told me the high winds had grounded the balloon for now. Saved.

Kailani wasn't too blue about it. The basic idea of Port Discovery is

*The restored 1854 sloop of war U.S.S. Constellation, the second U.S. Navy ship to bear that name, at its permanent berth at the west end of the Inner Harbor.*

learning through play, and she's all about play. The building's centerpiece is Mount Kidmore, a three-story jungle gym comprised of slides, tubes, rope ladders, net walkways, metal spiral staircases—all connecting the three floors at various points. In other words, it's a kid magnet, and mine were in there and vanished from view in an instant. For the next couple of hours Johnny and I took up stations around the building to figure out where they were going to pop out, with occasional forays into the thing to rescue Kailani, who got lost now and again when her older brother raced ahead.

Surrounding the jungle gym on all three floors were a variety of places to learn and play. There was a computer lab where kids could use programs to play games or make music; a conveyer belt widget machine into which you had to place different shapes in the correct places as they rolled by; an art room for creating all kinds of art projects; and, in one corner, the Space Time Travelator. In here was a dark and rather spooky exhibit about ancient Egypt. It included "Fatima's Bizarre Bizarro," where we lifted the lids of a series of wooden boxes and tried to identify the exotic spices within using only the sense of smell. In another area, two big brass dials let you turn a disc to match English letters to their hieroglyphic counterpart. I used charcoal and paper to etch my name in hieroglyphics. We pulled ourselves across the Nile on a sliding wooden bridge, against a backdrop of palms and stars, deserts and camels.

We could easily have spent all day at Port Discovery, but I had something even cooler planned—the ultimate Baltimore ride. Admittedly, this was outside the "kids choose" rule of the weekend, and also it's not something available to the public. But there are certain perks to this job, and one of them is to meet a lot of interesting people, and every now and then call in a favor. So I had done a few weeks earlier when I called Duff Hughes, president of Vane Brothers Company, and asked him if he had really meant it awhile back when he said he'd love to give my family a ride on one of his tugs. You bet, he said, and we set it up. We were to meet at the aquarium, so off we went, stopping by briefly to say hello to the harbor seals in their outdoor tank, then rounding the corner and there she was, the two push knees on her bow snugged up against the concrete pier: the *Mitzie Hughes*. Our ride was here.

"Whoa," Kaeo said when he saw her. "Whoa," we all agreed with him. How cool was this? A 60-foot, 800-horse tug waiting, just for us to go tootling around the harbor? Built in 1973 in Houma, La., the *Mitzie*

*Hughes* is one of Vane Brothers' 10 towboats and tugs that help bunker ships and move barges throughout the Bay and elsewhere. Deckhand Ross Gaither helped us onboard, and we headed for the bridge, where Captain Tommy Payne spun her on a dime quickly away from the pier and we were off, a giant among the powerboats, water taxis and sailboats scurrying around the water like bugs. The heck with the balloon—this 360-degree view from the tug's bridge was the best ever. "Yeah, for a view, it's okay," Payne agreed. We passed HarborView and looked for the reassuring sight of *Luna*'s mast, right where it belonged, and headed out into the no-nonsense, business end of the harbor. "Where do you want to go?" Payne asked us. Where to begin?

I had never been into Curtis Bay, so that's where we headed. "Hey, Tommy, what's this?" Kaeo asked, and Payne showed him how the radar worked. "That's us right there," he said. "See that barge there movin'?" He pointed out the window. "That's that. And that ship there (more pointing), that's this here." Minutes later, "Hey, Tommy, what are these?"

"That puts the electric to my flanking rudders, and these run the winches so I can pull the barges in and out."

"Hey, Tommy, what's that?"

"That's the Curtis Bay ore pier, and Curtis Bay Coal. And that's Bayside Coal, and the Hess oil dock."

"Hey, Tommy, what's this? . . ." And so it went for about an hour, kids and grown-ups alike peppering him with questions, his answers patient, generous and sometimes amused. Johnny finally achieved the weekend's goal of forgetting he was a grown-up when Payne offered him the chance to take the steering arm and guide *Mitzie Hughes* out of Curtis Bay and back toward the Inner Harbor. As we approached the aquarium pier, we thanked Payne for taking time on a Sunday afternoon to give us a ride. "Hey, you got me out of housework!" he laughed.

Even after that, the kids weren't yet done with the water. Right in front of the World Trade Center is a fleet of colorful pedal boats—the ultimate tourist candy—and they wanted to take one out in the worst way. Johnny and I tried to weasel out of it; after all, our kids are on the water nearly every day, and back at *Luna* they had their own dinghy to paddle anywhere they wanted. But there was no escaping it. As a kid's ride, the pedal boats are cool, especially the ones that look like dragons and are painted purple and green. Kaeo chose his perfect boat. Johnny, the boatyard owner and need-for-speed yacht racer, sighed deeply. "Do you think we could haul her, power spray her, tune her up just a little?"

After the *Mitzie Hughes*, it was a bit too grown-up to suddenly have to succumb to the orders of two demanding midget captains to pedal faster. "Hey, this is a lot like work," Johnny said. We let the kids take over, and in about 10 minutes they agreed with that assessment and headed in. From there, it was a half-hour walk home, with a quick stop at the carousel for some caramel corn and yet another ride, this one on the back of a painted horse.

---

Monday morning dawned—another perfect, bright autumn day. We snagged an easy, delicious breakfast of coffee, juice, muffins and pastries at the marina's Barista Espresso Cafe, and set out on foot again for what will always be my one true love of the Inner Harbor—the National Aquarium in Baltimore. On cold winter days I can spend hours in the warm dampness of its rainforest, looking for scarlet ibises and sloths and listening to the tropical music of the birds. On hot summer days I can sit

*The U.S. Coast Guard cutter* Taney, *a survivor of the 1941 attack on Pearl Harbor and now a museum ship, awaits visitors at its mooring on Pier 5, east of the aquarium.*

mesmerized in the cool dimness of the shark tank, watching the silent, constant passage of fierce pointed snouts and leathery bodies and feathery gills.

Of course, that was before I took the kids there. Now when we go it's a full-on sprint from start to finish, a sort of Evelyn Wood speed-reading interpretation of everything this remarkable place has to offer. My kids ricochet through the aquarium like pinballs, bouncing off of one amazing sight after another, slightly overwhelmed and emphatically astounded. Perennial favorites (and reason for stopping more than 30 seconds) are the electric eel, the brilliantly colored poison tree frogs, the gigantic groupers—and of course the rays, sharks and sea turtles.

This time was no different, except the place was full of little bobbing shark's heads, since all the kids got a little visor in the image of Bruce, the meat-addicted great white shark from the movie *Finding Nemo*. Despite our enforced haste, we spied a green sea turtle missing a front flipper and learned that it had suffered an infection in the wild. When it was brought to the aquarium, the turtle's flipper had to be amputated. Even

*Another Federal Hill view, with Inner Harbor Marina in the foreground, excursion ships on the west bulkhead and the U.S.S.* Constellation *at its mooring on the far side.*

with all that, it was still a bewitching, mysterious animal, full of grace. We identified a roughtail stingray and a cownose ray, a lemon shark and a sand tiger shark, and we watched the slow, steady fluttering of a nurse shark's gills as it rested on the tank's bottom, not three feet away from us. We laughed at the quick, busy travels of the lookdown fish, which always remind me of stock traders rushing to some bell. We visited the seahorse exhibit once more, stunned at the ethereal magic of these creatures that seem like they should spring from fairy tales.

Finally we took in the dolphin show (another perennial favorite), and this time was fun because Kaeo was old enough to really understand the trainers and play along, identifying the dolphins' signature whistles and spotting the new calves. Watching the dolphins, their grace and perception, their pure power and joy at leaping and rifling through the water, I always forget I'm a grown-up.

It was a lovely day for a boat ride, and at last, the kids (and grown-ups) were tired of running—and walking. We grabbed a water taxi and headed back to the marina, where *Luna* was waiting to take us home. Behind us, the HiFlyer soared over Port Discovery. "Can we go up in that?" my daughter asked me, one more time. "Next time," I told her, and I really did mean it. Next time.

---

This article first appeared in *Chesapeake Bay Magazine* in July 2004. Wendy Mitman Clarke was then executive editor of the magazine and is now an editor-at-large and a frequent contributor.

*Severn River:*

## World Enough & Time

6

*The Severn River above Annapolis has a destination for every boater and, for those lucky enough to live nearby, time enough to do it.*

*by Jody Argo Schroath*

Scene One: The sky is pale blue above a lazy cone of early morning cumulus, and I am in the galley carefully crushing saltines, which perversely explode into the air creating a fine fallout of crumbs that settle into the cracks and crevices of the stove and onto the cabin sole. It's a Saturday in mid-July, and I'm mixing up crabcakes to be cooked on the stern-mounted grill at anchor this evening somewhere on the Severn River.

Scene Two: Fall is on its way, and I am stepping onto the boat with a Trader Joe's bag containing the day's menu for a meal to be consumed on the Severn River: small tubs of hummus, pitted kalamata olives, sheep's milk feta and stuffed grape leaves. A *ficelle* of French bread sticks out of the bag. A ripe cantaloupe comes on board with me too. Unknown to me just then, it will spend the day quietly rolling up and down the galley floor as my daughter Kris and I cruise up the Severn to her favorite anchorage at the top of Hopkins Creek. Happily, we'll find its pungent sweet flavor undiminished by its peregrinations.

Scene Three: This time it's a weekday morning in late May, and the cockpit of the boat is still heavy with dew as I stand in the galley, orchestrating the construction of sandwiches—caraway-seeded rye bread, thinly sliced rare roast beef, finely cut onion and horseradish—for lunch with good friends on the hook somewhere on the Severn River.

Three scenes and three separate destinations, all on the same short river. I could easily have thought of more, one for each time I've taken a boat up beyond the bridges. And I'm a relative newcomer to this area. What about the others, the ones lucky enough to spend their lives along the river itself? And what about those others, perhaps a little less lucky by some measures, who spend their lives below the bridges, but within easy reach? How many scenes and how many destinations could they compose? The Severn is that kind of river. Not that it gets much respect on the Bay in general. It's always all about Annapolis. But if the Severn gets overshadowed by the star power of its principal port, so much the better for the rest of us. We know beyond a shadow of a doubt that the Severn above the bridges, with its high wooded bluffs, deep creeks, pocket beaches, party sandbars, drowned islands and jaw-dropping homes, is one of the most beautiful, accessible and boater-friendly places on the Bay, east or west, north or south. It's Ozzie and Harriet, the one percent, Robin Hood, arms dealers, Capuchin monks and a Paris cafe all rolled into one. And all you have to do to find it is slip beyond the two bridges. I do it all the time.

———

Take Scene One, for example. My husband Rick and I have invited a few friends to come out for a late-day cruise on this hot summer Saturday. We could join the throng of boats in the Bay, sailing out and then sailing in, but instead we decide to travel up the Severn and search out a cool place to anchor before returning in the early evening. We set off at about four, but the wind is fitful and the sail is painfully slow and hot. Eventually, we surrender to the ease of motoring, but stay out of the creeks, which are our usual destinations but now are likely to be breathless and buggy. Instead, after we reach Round Bay, we head west, letting go the anchor along the north shore of Little Round Bay near Long Point, hoping to catch any soft evening southerly that may find its way in off the Bay. We get more than we bargained for. A passing squall briefly whips up the bay before passing rainless into the east. We put the crabcakes on the grill just as the sun begins its long summer exit and are through with dinner and bustling back home before the stars have time to take the stage.

The structure of the Severn River is straight forward, running north-west from its mouth for about 10 miles in a fairly straight line. The channel too is straightforward, running nearly shore to shore from its mouth to Indian Landing, always accepting the usual shoal areas around points. Where there are exceptions, as in a particularly large shoal off Brewer Point, the way is well marked. Along the river's brief course, a remarkable dozen or so navigable creeks shoot off to left and right of the main stem. The river's mouth is formed on the north by Greenbury Point, with its famous old radio towers and infamous long shoal—marked by flashing red "4"—and on the south by Tolly Point, with its equally infamous shoal—marked by flashing green "1AH". This lower section of the river needs no introduction, as Annapolis Roads leads into Annapolis harbor, with Back and Spa creeks below the bridges offering shelter to hundreds of recreational vessels, both resident and transient, and Weems Creek between the bridges offering shelter to a good many more. You can follow the river past Annapolis along the Naval Academy bulkhead, then under the two fixed bridges—the Naval Academy and the U.S. 50/301 bridge—

*A small cottage near the Severn River's Indian Landing. Preceding pages: A sailboat gliding up the Severn River with homes dotting the high bluffs on shore.*

before it widens into Round Bay and Little Round Bay about six and a half miles upriver. Then the river narrows once again and makes a slight jog to the west at The Narrows. Here one finally loses sight of the bridges. Two miles later, the navigable river comes to an end, just beyond Indian Landing. It's a lovely run. The river and its creeks are bounded everywhere by high wooded bluffs. They are also highly developed with homes of every size and description, though many share their steep slopes with mature red oaks and towering tulip poplars.

––––––––––––

Take Hopkins Creek, for example, our destination in Scene Two and Kris's favorite anchorage. It's late September, and the sun's bite is finally beginning to fade. Our Middle Eastern smorgasbord is stowed in the refrigerator, and our dogs are strapped into their life preservers. Kris and I head out of Port Annapolis into Back Creek and then make a beeline across the harbor to head upriver. We have only a few hours before we need to be back for dinner with friends. We won't have time to visit any of our other favorite spots, but that won't prevent us from thinking about them as we pass them by. I throttle back the sailing cat's twin 29s, and Kris raises the jib to catch the smart southeast breeze that soon begins to nudge us gently upriver. Perfect. Shortly after clearing the second bridge, we pass the first of the Severn's upriver tributaries, Cool Spring Cove. This small jewel on the starboard shore is guarded inside by a long rock jetty that juts from a spit of land. A small white cottage, only a few feet from the water, nestles into a protecting canopy of trees that have clearly kept it safe over the years from storms galloping up the river. The depth going into the cove reads between 13 and 15 feet and about 9 feet going around and behind the jetty, with the deepest water to be found to port of the six-knot speed marker. Inside are a few homes, mostly hidden in the trees, and a few boats, including a battered old lifeboat. It is small. A boat could anchor here in a pinch, but not, perhaps, a very big boat. I had passed the cove many times over the years without going in because the entrance looked daunting and the dimensions cramped. Finally, on a chill fall morning while Rick and I were making a trip upriver in a center-console, with the mist still lying over the warm water, we decided to look in. We were enchanted by the little cottage and the old lifeboat, and we found the entrance much easier than it looked on the chart.

Passing the cove now with Kris, I point to the imposing residence that looks down over the cove's entrance and out the river from a steep bluff. That house was built in the 1920s by an arms dealer, I say, and then became a monastery for Capuchin monks. They left in the 1970s, and the house sat empty for 30 years, looking grim and haunting the dreams of fanciful young boaters who passed beneath its shadow. About 10 years ago, it was bought by the owner of Phillips Seafood, who reduced its 20-some monk-size bedrooms to a more comfortable seven, with eight bathrooms, 11 fireplaces and a nine-car garage.

A few minutes later, we reach Round Bay. Since we're heading for Hopkins Creek, which will put us in the lee of the land and therefore out of the wind, we drop the jib and motor west into Little Round Bay and south of St. Helena Island—possibly home to a speakeasy during Prohibition, and just as possibly not. Hopkins is a splendid little creek with a long sandbar closing off all but a small entrance channel. The deep water passes nerve-rackingly close to the sand spit and then curves around behind it before continuing along generally in the center. The area behind the spit makes a fine anchorage—protected, but still open enough to catch a little breeze on a hot night. Kris and I, however, proceed to the end, passing down the hallway of tall trees and cliffs to the little marsh at the end, no more than half a mile in all. It should be late enough in the year to anchor here with impunity: not too hot and not too buggy. If it had been either one of those, we likely would have decided to anchor in Hopkins' sister creek instead. Maynadier (pronounced –deer at the end) and Hopkins share an entrance off the south shore of Little Round Bay, with Maynadier splitting off to starboard behind Mathiers Point. The creek curls around another point then opens into a perfect little bay, with depths of 8 to 10 feet and enough room for a small flotilla to swing at anchor and still not crowd the homes that populate the section of shore that is not marsh. Yes, here too there is marsh, so you can have your summer breeze and wildlife watching too. There is even a small slalom course set up for water-skiing.

This early fall day, Kris and I have the head of Hopkins Creek to ourselves. With the anchor down, Skipper stands at the bow, whipping his head from side to side, as he watches a pair of blue herons chase each other over the top of the marsh grass and finally argue their way out of the creek altogether. Kris and I watch the birds as we sit at the table in the cockpit, making short work of the hummus and feta before settling down to our dented cantaloupe. We while away a few more minutes over our iced teas before pulling up anchor and motoring back down river. We arrive home in plenty of time for dinner.

That's the charm of the Severn. It doesn't take a lot of time to have fun. You can go up the same river, but have a different experience every time, depending on the time of year, day of the week, and choice of creek. What could be more modern? Or economical in these days of high fuel prices? Even landlubbers love a cruise up the Severn. They find it unthreatening and beautiful. Best of all, perhaps, they are not obliged to sleep on the boat! That's a very appealing scenario for the boatowner in some cases, as well.

---

This brings us to Scene Three. The refrigerator is well stocked with roast beef and horseradish sandwiches when my guests arrive. They are dear friends from Ohio. They both grew up, went to school together, married and raised their children in the same small town, about 50 miles inland from Lake Erie. It's a gently rolling land of haystacks, apples, strawberries, silver-queen corn and big-boy tomatoes. It has no boats. "We're game for anything," they tell me on arriving. But I know better—or at least I'm pretty sure I do. I've already decided that we'll go

*Sailboats coming and going under the Naval Academy bridge.*

up the Severn and have a picnic. But first I feel obliged to give them a quick run up Spa Creek as far as the bridge so they can see Annapolis from the water—a thing everyone on earth should do at least once, I figure. We exit the slip with reasonable grace and head out Back Creek and into Annapolis harbor to avoid the Horn Point shoal. Immediately, a trawler the size of small iceberg jostles past us, anxious to be on its way. We roll over the wake it has left carelessly behind. Caught off guard, my friends are suddenly nervous and grasp the cockpit coaming tight. I say something inane but, I hope, reassuring, and we settle down again. It's a busy day out here, but not terribly busy, because it's still early in the season. We pick our way through a flock of small sailboats and roll over more wakes before we turn to follow the Academy bulkhead toward City Dock. Fifteen minutes later, our tour complete, we are all measurably relieved as I turn left out of Spa Creek to follow the river up and under the bridges. Not that there isn't wake here as well, but it is more predictable, with boats either going up or coming down the river rather than going every which way. We have the sails up now too, which steadies the motion considerably. I can feel the tension easing with every minute. We have a beautiful sail!

Passing by, we look up Chase Creek, which is just beyond Cool Springs Cove. My husband Rick, who is not with us on this trip, loves Chase's split personality, I tell them. The creek's right branch curls around a small shoal and then squeezes through a narrow passage to open into a lovely small cove with a depth of about seven feet. Homes cling to the high bluffs that line the shore, nearly lost in the trees. There's just room enough for a boat to swing at anchor, completely protected from whatever might be happening outside. The left branch, by contrast, is full of moored boats as well as Pines on the Severn's community beach and slips. One day, I explain, Rick and I watched a well-found sloop ghost up to the dock under sail, drop its main and come to a dead stop head to wind, perfectly positioned. Wow, Rick had whispered. Someday.

Passing Chase Creek, my friends and I run under the wind as far as the top of Round Bay—far enough for their first outing, I think—then turn into the wind and drop the sails. A long beat downriver doesn't seem like a good idea. I have them on my side now, and I don't want to lose them. Besides, it's already time for lunch. So I make a short detour to show them Little Round Bay and St. Helena before turning back. Along the leeward shore, where the deep water curves in toward shore at the former entrance to Brewer Pond, we pass a nice old Pearson with the anchor down, its occupant stretched out in the cockpit, deep in a book. They are definitely on my side now. This is nice. We round Brewer Point, staying well off to avoid the shoal and keeping flashing green "5" on our right, before turning into the entrance to Brewer Creek.

As we drift inside, I point to the right, where the dark brown homes of Sherwood Forest rise three deep in some places up the steep and deeply wooded hillside. This land was developed in the 1920s as summer cottages, I tell them, and was named after the Sherwood Forest of Robin Hood, as you might have guessed. They're certainly not summer cottages anymore, my friends reply, clearly impressed. We soon reach the end of the creek, so I turn the boat around and we head back out, turning right and then right again into the creek immediately below it—Clements. I continue my description: A second parcel of land was developed at the same time and located next door, I say, but this one was named Epping Forest, which is located near the original Sherwood Forest, so the Robin Hood thing works here too. But each is very much its own community, I continue, with governing organizations, and in Epping Forest's case, its own summer camp. Looking up, we can see narrow ribbons of road descending steeply from the homes along the top to the water below.

This is where we're going to stop for lunch, I tell them, pointing to one of the Naval Academy mooring balls in a small cove off the creek's southern shore. I slip the engines into neutral and go forward to snag a mooring. The Naval Academy keeps these mooring balls on some of the creeks as hurricane holes for their boats, I explain. When they are not using them, they are available for anyone to use. Now, I say, if you'll open up the cockpit table, we'll have lunch. And we do. A light breeze blows up the creek from the river, and we pass a happy hour eating sandwiches and polishing off glasses of cold lemonade. It's mid-afternoon when we retrieve our line from the mooring ball and then motor back into the river. Reaching Annapolis harbor once again, we pick our way back across the busy stretch of water to flashing red "2E" and flashing green "1E", which mark the entrance to Back Creek, and home. We are all satisfied with the day's adventure, and the Severn River and two brand-new fans.

---

The Severn River's biggest fans are quite naturally the people who live there. Take a ride upriver any day of the week during the summer and you'll see them. Search the community beaches and you'll find them sitting in slingback chairs along the shore, watching their children splash and play in the water. Scan the hundreds of private docks and piers, and you'll find children and dogs playing and people fishing, sunning or reading. Watching three laughing little girls jumping off the swim platform of a docked boat on Chase Creek one day, I thought it would almost be worth growing up again as long as I could do it on the Severn River.

There is an old cliché that if you sit long enough in a sidewalk cafe in Paris, everyone you know will eventually walk past. On the Severn, that Paris cafe is the fuel dock at Smith's Marina in Browns Cove off Little Round Bay. Hang around long enough and everyone on the river will eventually come by. On a summer day, the parade of boats coming into Smith's fuel dock seems unending. Earlier this year, Rick and I stopped at Smith's for only a few minutes, but it was long enough to meet four separate boats captained and crewed by women who were out for an afternoon spin on the river, as much at home in their boats as their back-yards—no doubt because they were one and the same. Smith's Marina

*Homes atop a bluff overlooking a large catamaran on a mooring on the Severn, just below the Naval Academy bridge.*

has been in the same place in the same family since it was established in 1936 as a boat rental and bait business. This summer they are opening a grand new building for the ship's store, office and restrooms.

---

Epilogue: It's Memorial Day weekend, and I'm running late for a trip up the Severn. I'm so late, I don't even have time to do anything about lunch. But I don't really care. I'm going to make the trip with a colleague in his little 1960 runabout, which is painted bright orange and blue and has fins. The engine is not quite as old, a 75-hp Evinrude, but it's decked out in black and white racing checks. We are going to look pretty cool going up the river! He and I meet at Lake Ogleton, where we launch the boat, then head out across Annapolis harbor. We bounce and bobble across the wakes of a hundred boats. Everybody must be out on the water today, I think. Finally, we clear the bridges and the water smooths considerably. We begin to duck into one creek after another on our way upriver—Cool Springs Cove, Chase, Saltworks, Clements, Brewer. Every creek, every beach, every piece of the river is full of people and boats of every age and description. On Chase Creek, a family from Leesburg, Va., on a trailer cruiser is enjoying their own quiet swimming hole. On Clements Creek, *Caper*, *Winona*, *Ugly Duckling* and *Sunrise* ride on moorings. On Luce Creek, *Twill* and *Miss Trish Won* lie at Navy moorings while raft-ups are forming nearby. Beyond Round Bay, we look up Valentine and Plum creeks then Forked Creek, home to the Severn's only eastern shore marina, Severna Park Yacht Basin. Forked Creek is also home to some very big houses. Out of Forked Creek, we turn north again and slow down to pass through The Narrows. Here the river feels like a set from a 1950s live-action sitcom—*Ozzie and Harriet* with boats. Look, I say, there's Ozzie watching David and Ricky building an Optimist pram in the backyard. Harriet's probably down at Smith's filling up the family Chris-Craft.

Another mile upriver and we reach the islands. On First Island, a small platoon of runabouts is pulled up along the sand. This is a favorite rendezvous because the island is surrounded by deep water nearly to its sandy shore. Second Island, just off Indian Landing, is empty save for an old deserted cottage that is slowly toppling into the water. The remnants of Third Island can be seen beyond Indian Landing. Beyond Third Island the river shallows quickly, making a final turn before ending in the freshwater Severn Run. We circle First Island and head back down-river. It's time for lunch. We follow the parade into Smith's Marina. We walk into the ship's store, and pick out two ice cream bars and a couple of bottles of water. It's a far cry from fresh grilled crabcakes and roast beef sandwiches, but it couldn't have tasted better. We climb into the boat and head back onto the river. The sun is hot now, but the wind we create as we speed downriver makes it tolerable. Reaching the harbor, we turn off to take a turn up Ego Alley, then pick our way through the anarchy of holiday boat traffic to Lake Ogleton.

As I sit at the ramp, waiting for my colleague to return with the boat trailer, I get to thinking about Captain John Smith. No doubt he was a great man and a prodigious explorer, but the Severn River is where he went wrong. Smith seems to have explored nearly every nook and cranny on the Bay, but he never went up the Severn. His mistake, I think to myself. If he had, he'd have picked out a homestead and settled down to live happily ever after. And right now, his great-great-great-great-great-grandson would be walking over to Ozzie and Harriet's house up at The Narrows to see if he could borrow an outboard for the old family shallop.

This article first appeared in *Chesapeake Bay Magazine* in July 2012. Jody Argo Schroath is senior editor of the magazine and editor of its annual *Guide to Cruising Chesapeake Bay.*

*Kent Island:*

# 7

## Crossing Kent

*In search of the quiet side of Kent Island, by boat
and bike . . . and sore tuckus.*

by T. F. Sayles

The deeply tanned waterman, coiling line as he sat
in the open cockpit of his 20-foot Wellcraft—clearly
once a sport boat, now just as clearly a workboat—
flashed a smile and returned my wave. But his
eyes asked the obvious questions: Dang it all, am I
going to have to pull another one of these weekend
wackos off the mud? What on earth is this knucklehead
doing so far up the creek in that big boat? Doesn't he realize
how shallow it is up here?

Yes, he realized that; his depthsounder had been making that very
point, in its shrill way, for the last hundred yards or so. And now the
knucklehead (he being I, you may have guessed) was just looking for a
good place among the moored workboats to turn around. I had been
carefully motoring up Thompson Creek, a shallow but still powerboat-
friendly arm of Cox Creek on the Eastern Bay side of Kent Island. My
destination: Kent Manor Inn, which I'd assumed would clearly show itself
on the west side of the creek. It had not. The inn itself, though a fairly
large and imposing 19th-century manor house, was hidden by the trees;
and because the tide was quite high (at least that part went according to
plan), the inn's dock was barely visible above the water.

I figured all this out as I retraced my path downstream and

approached the inn from the north, this time getting a second opinion from my iPhone and seeing more clearly where Kent Manor Drive ended—relative to where I, the blue dot, was on the creek. I chuckled to myself, thinking the blue dot should have been labeled, "You, knucklehead, are here." And that could have meant two things: not only where I was on the map, but also that I had arrived at the first and most important destination of this adventure. My goal was to see the side of Kent Island that you don't see if you stay "downtown"—at the Narrows, that bustling nexus of boats, bulkheads, boatyards, marinas, bars, restaurants, restaurants and restaurants that separates the island from Grasonville, Md., and the Eastern Shore proper. Not that there's anything wrong with a bustling nexus, mind you. I've partaken of most of the pleasures that the Narrows has to offer—meals at most of the restaurants, slips at the marinas, a dark-and-stormy too many at Red Eye's Dock Bar.

But the idea this time was to explore the not-so-beaten paths of Kent Island. And those paths, it turned out, in keeping with my modus operandi of late, happened to be bike trails—specifically, the east-west Cross Island Trail, which runs from the Bay-side beach at Terrapin Park, in the shadow of the Chesapeake Bay Bridge, past the town of Stevensville, and then across to Kent Island Narrows; and the South Island Trail, which parallels Route 8, running down the southern neck of the island from Matapeake State Park to Romancoke. And by staying at the Kent Manor Inn for two nights and Bay Bridge Marina for one, I'd be bicycle striking distance from the trails' west and north termini, respectively, and from Stevensville.

Phase one of the trip, crossing from Annapolis to the back side of Kent Island, was a much rougher slog than I'd expected. I'd been overly focused on two other bugaboos—thunderstorms and shallow water—so I'd been less than attentive to the sea conditions that afternoon. From a weather standpoint, it being high season for afternoon thunderstorms, a morning crossing would have been ideal. But it would've been the worst time to go in terms of tide. And, given the skinny water I was heading into on Thompson Creek, I chose the latter of the devils. That is, I'd rather risk getting rained on than running aground. In those terms alone, the gamble paid off. I neither got rained on nor ran aground, though I certainly flirted with the latter by overshooting the inn's dock. Conditions on the upper Bay that afternoon, though, were not particularly civilized—with three- and four-foot crosswise seas pummeling me all the way from the mouth of the Severn to Bloody Point. On the upside, these are the conditions that an Albin 28 is made for. I wouldn't have dreamed of crossing on a day like this in one of the Chesapeake Boating Club's smaller boats (and they'd have likely forbidden it). But the Albin? Pfft! Not a problem. Bouncy, yes. Noisy, sure. Rollercoaster, oh yeah. But all of it very much in stride—and all at the boat's seemingly unshakable cruising speed of 12 to 13 knots.

Things calmed down considerably, of course, as soon as I turned the corner into Eastern Bay, and by the time I'd reached the wide shared mouth of Cox and Shipping creeks, a couple of miles above Romancoke, things had gotten downright civilized—serene even, although the bruise-colored western sky concerned me a little. Maybe that's what had me distracted enough to putter right past the Kent Manor Inn's dock without realizing it. After the careful U-turn upstream, I worked my way back to what was, in the satellite view of my iPhone's Google map, clearly the inn property—an enormous house, a parking lot and a pool at the end of Kent Manor Drive, with a sizable L dock reaching about 100 feet into the creek. But from the creek it was all easy to miss. The house is mostly obscured by trees, and the dock, at this hour and on this day, was next to

*The author's Albin 28,* Venture, *in its slip at Bay Bridge Marina, with his bike alongside. Preceding pages: A shady, wooded area of the South Island trail.*

invisible, being both unoccupied and nearly submerged in the unusually high water. Indeed, if it hadn't been for the half-dozen plastic Adirondack chairs bolted to the dock's outer arm, seemingly perched on the water itself, I might have missed it on the second pass too. But I didn't, and soon I was tying up at the outside corner of the L . . . and explaining myself to a gregarious teenager named A.J. Within minutes of my landing, the young man had come sauntering down the dock, asking cheerfully if I was taking shelter there because of the looming storm. "No," I said, "Actually, I'm staying here tonight, and tomorrow night. At the inn." At which point, since I still couldn't actually see an inn, it occurred to me that I still might not have found it. "This is the Kent Manor Inn, right?" I asked. "I mean, this is their dock?"

"Yessir, it is." A.J. said, "We saw you coming in, and my dad said I should come down and see if everything was alright. We thought maybe you were coming in because of the storm. . . . We live right over there," he said, pointing to a house a hundred yards away, just upstream from the dock. "My dad works for the inn, he does the maintenance. My mom works there too." All this was volunteered, and quickly followed by lots of questions about the boat. "That'd be a great boat for fishing!" he said, eyeing the open cockpit. "Do you take it out fishing?" No, I told him, mostly just cruising and exploring, not a lot of fishing. "You don't?" he asked incredulously. "Man, I would if I had a boat like that. I'd be fishing every day!"

"Yeah, I said. I have friends who say the same thing. They say it's a waste of a perfectly good fishing boat."

"Oh, no, I didn't mean that!" A.J. backpedaled. "I like to just be out on a boat too! Just be out there on the water. That's cool, just being out there, doing . . . you know, whatever." From the way he said "out there on the water," with something approaching reverence, it was clear to me he had a good bit of Thompson Creek water in his veins. He was a waterman waiting to happen, I thought—somewhat ruefully, of course, because nowadays that's not the most promising career path for A.J.

After A.J. said good-bye and headed back to his house, I finished securing the boat, then wrestled my bike out of the cockpit and onto the dock. (Note to self: For Pete's sake, maybe you should get a lighter bike for these purposes? One of these days you're going to pop a back muscle heaving around this heavy, fat-tire cruiser.) Walking the bike off the dock, past a gazebo and across a footbridge traversing a narrow finger of marsh, jammed tight with phragmites, I got my first good look at the inn. It's a big old manor house, built around 1820, nestled in among mature trees and enormous shrubs and situated sidelong to the creek. Its two-story open-air front porch, running the width of the house, looks north across a circle drive. In the back, a long glassed-in porch and sprawling multilevel deck face south, looking out on a wide sweep of lawn, the foot-bridge, a pool and a large single-story octagonal outbuilding for large-group meetings, parties and receptions. Weddings and conferences are the name of the game here—the former accounting for most of the week-end activity and the latter for the weekdays. Indeed, my original plan had been to stay here on a Friday and Saturday, but with a wedding booked for that weekend, there were no guest rooms available for Saturday. Or the next Saturday. Or the next or the next. But no problem; Thursday and Friday worked too.

The first order of business, once I'd found a place to lock up my bike, was to check in—though here the process has a more personal flavor to it than the term "check in" implies. Inn manager Amy Fowler, the very person I'd spoken with when I called a week earlier to reserve the room, invited me to have a seat at her desk while she checked me in, found a room key for me and gave me the rundown. That included a phone number to call (A.J.'s parents, it turned out) if I needed any after-hours assistance. That alone—that there is an "after hours"—tells you something about the place. With 24 guest rooms and wedding and con-ference facilities, it's hardly a bed-and-breakfast. But it's not a hotel either. I like that.

Given the long day and the rough ride across the Bay, I was tempted to just take a shower and spend the rest of the evening in my very large and very English room with a book in my lap and my iPod on shuffle. But I was also hungry, so I decided to first hop on the bike and go forag-ing for dinner—thinking, incorrectly, that the inn's restaurant was open only for brunch on Sundays. It is, in fact, open from Thursday through Sunday, for lunch and dinner, plus Sunday brunch. Silly me. If only I could read.

So off I went on the bike, down the long, bending, tree-lined drive, then right on Route 8, then right again just shy of Route 50, along the ac-cess road that leads past a Kmart and then to Thompson Creek shopping center. This, I knew from experience (I used to live out this way), would be my prime foraging ground. I wasn't sure what I wanted—just something interesting, yet reasonably healthful. That latter bit, by my definition, ruled out some of the obvious choices: pizza, KFC, pizza, Mexican, Cracker Barrel. That left only a bar and grill, a sushi place, a Food Lion and . . . wait, sushi? Here? On Kent Island? Yes, my eyes had not deceived me. Right there, just a few doors down from the Food Lion, was Ichiban Japanese Restaurant and Sushi Bar. Culinary quandary averted. Cucumber roll.

Oshinko roll. California roll. Me happy. Indeed I was so happy about this unexpected turn of events that I didn't even mind getting rained on, torrentially, on the ride back to the Kent Manor Inn. It helped prepare me for the equally torrential shower I took back at the room.

------

The next morning I happily frittered away a few hours with coffee and scones and fresh fruit on the inn's broad front porch, waiting for the spitty weather to clear. It finally did, around noon, at which point I unlocked the bike and fired up the iPhone GPS. In addition to its built-in GPS, the phone was now loaded with an application called Trails, which, like some marine navigation apps, would record my track that day. This was hardly vital to the day's mission—a round trip to Kent Narrows and

*A view of the Jetty Restaurant and dock bar on Kent Narrows from the Cross Island trail.*

back on the east-west Cross Island Trail—but I liked the idea of having "data" from the trip: total mileage, average speed, elevation changes, and of course the track itself, represented by a bright red line on the map. I had imagined myself back at the inn that night, sitting on the porch, sipping scotch and reviewing the day's adventure. This, however, will be the last you hear of this technological experiment, because, like all navigation apps, this one is fraught with opportunities for user error—and a week or so later I found one of those opportunities and took full advantage of it. That is, I deleted the entire day's track with one ill-advised tap of the NO, DON'T SAVE button, followed by another ill-advised tap of the YES, I'M SURE button. I also discovered that phone's battery is not up to an entire day's worth of unplugged GPS tracking. Unlike the car and boat, the bike has no 12-volt outlet to help keep the damn thing charged up. . . . But I've let all that go, because, after all, this is about boating and biking, not about the shortcomings of shirt-pocket technology.

Tim, do you hear me? Let. It. Go.

If you're the least bit familiar with Route 50 on Kent Island, you know it's not especially pedestrian- or bicycle-friendly, least of all here at the eastern foot of the Bay Bridge. So the first part of the day's trek, crossing said highway by way of the Route 8 overpass, was far and away the most dangerous and nerve-racking 10 minutes of the day. Once north of 50, though, it's only a quarter mile to the first traffic light, where you may turn right onto Main Street, into Stevensville proper, or left on Skipjack Parkway, then through Chesapeake Business Park, to find the west end of the Cross Island Trail. On this end, it is not at all linear; it is in fact the meandering trail system for Terrapin Beach Park (owned by Queen Anne's County), which is nestled against the Bay immediately north of the Bay Bridge, with a thin half-mile strip of sand beach (a very popular *area de pesca* and picnic spot for Latino families) and 276 acres of marsh, woods, meadows and former farmland.

After exploring the park trails for a couple of hours, I was ready to head east. But rather than go straight out the trail, I went back through the business park to Route 8—for a visit to Stevensville, a town that had never been more to me than a name on a highway sign. As many times as I've zoomed through here on Route 50, I've never seen the town itself, and never realized how old and appealing and, well, town-like it is. From the light at Route 8, it's just a quarter-mile or so to the center of town, or at least what feels like the center of town, anyway: the skewed intersection of East Main Street, Cockey Lane and Love Point Road. Here you find the greatest concentration of the town's historic buildings: namely, a beautiful old 1902 bank building, a tiny mid-19th-century post office (headquarters of the Kent Island Heritage Society), an even tinier 1902 railroad passenger depot, tucked away behind an artfully shabby antiques store kept company by an old wood-planked B&O Railroad caboose, and the post-and-plank Cray House, built in 1809 by a ship's carpenter.

There's also an attractive cluster of genteel businesses here—the aforementioned antiques store, called Paris Grey Cottage, artists' studios and galleries, a gourmet pastry shop called Peace of Cake, and, occupying a massive and beautiful red-brick building that clearly had once been a church, Ye Olde Church House Antiques. Presiding quietly and confidently over all this at the northwest corner of the intersection, across from the old post office, is the Rustico Restaurant and Wine Bar. It being early afternoon and there being plenty of daylight left for my trip to the Narrows and back, I decided to give it a try—and I'm very glad I did. Under the care of a sweet and attentive young waitress named Mary, I had a cup of cream of crab soup (perfect touch of sherry), an appetizer of Pomodori Verdi (fried green tomatoes topped with marinara and buffalo mozzarella) and a house salad with shrimp. And a lovely glass of Tuscan chianti, Castello Banfi to be exact.

But now it was time to test a shortcut I had discovered on the map that morning. It appeared that if I went a few blocks north on Love Point Road (a mini 19th-century architecture tour in its own right), turned right on Lowery Road then left on State Street, I would find, at the very end of State Street, a cut-through to the bike trail. And sure enough, there it was. This is the beginning of the trail's best part, actually, a long and mostly uninterrupted three miles from Stevensville to Piney Creek, just west of the Narrows. And the best of the best is the first (western-most) mile or so—a long, straight stretch of pavement, easily 10 feet wide and deeply shaded inside a 150-wide strip of mature woods. This is also the part that is so obviously, given its straightness and flat grade, a converted rail bed—the same rail bed, in fact (that of the Queen Anne's Railroad) that ran to the tiny depot in Stevensville. From there the rail line turned north, ending at the long-gone Love Point ferry landing.

The other end of the Queen Anne's line, I'd read somewhere, was Lewes, Del., and as I pedaled along this shady straightaway, across a lovely wooden bridge at Cox Creek and then back into the woods again, I couldn't help but think how great it would be if the bike path too went all the way to Lewes. . . .

Or, I reconsidered a bit later as the bike's seat began to feel less and less hospitable, maybe that wouldn't be so great on this bike. Today I was relearning what I'd learned the previous summer in hilly Occoquan, Va.—that a beach cruiser like this, with its fat tires, heavy frame, commodious seat and three paltry gears, is not ideal for either long distances or hilly terrain. For the first mile or so it's great, but after that it gets more and more like pedaling a Barcalounger.

This increasingly occupied my thoughts as I approached the east end of the trail, skirting Route 50, and then plunging into another woodsy mile before Piney Creek. It wasn't that I was sore or fatigued. Not yet. It was just that I knew that every foot I traveled in that direction was a foot I'd have to travel to get back to the other end of the island. But, fiddledee-dee, I told myself, I'll worry about that later, after a nice dinner at the relatively new Bridges Restaurant, one the few establishments on the Narrows that I had not yet sampled.

That last woodsy bit of trail emerges from the trees at the foot of another wooden bridge, this one over Piney Creek, and now closer than

*A B&O Railroad caboose that resides at the Stevensville train station along the Queen Anne's Railroad.*

ever to Route 50—indeed, barely a hundred feet from the westbound lanes. There the trail loses its secluded feel altogether, though it remains civilized and well segregated from the car traffic. At the east end of the defunct outlet shopping center, the trail turns left down Piney Narrows Road, ending where the road ends, at the county's Chesapeake Exploration Center. But it also continues straight, past Piney Narrows Road, under the highway at the foot of the new Kent Narrows bridge and, finally, across the Narrows on the old bridge. This last bit, across the bridge, isn't as perilous as it may sound to anyone who's driven it; indeed, it's reasonably safe, thanks to a well marked bike lane alongside the single westbound car lane.

I had a splendid meal at Bridges Restaurant—and not only because I was in a seat that, unlike the one I'd been on much of the day, was flat and considerably wider than my tush. That had something to do with it, but so did the perfect summer temperature (about 80 degrees and low humidity), and the tremendous 180-degree view of the Narrows, and the beautiful pan-seared crabcake, served with slabs of fried green tomato and fresh asparagus. I'd have loved to linger here longer, but, according to my iPhone's weather app, that would be a mistake, unless I wanted to get caught in the line of thunderstorms that was now moving through Frederick. Speaking of the iPhone, this was also the one and only time I saw the red line that I'd etched on the map with my Trails program. A week later, when I went to have another look, I somehow deleted it, and—

No, never mind, I said I wouldn't mention that again.

There's no need to go into great detail about the return trip, except to say it was very much like the eastbound trip, only backwards, and that I beat the thunderstorm to Kent Manor Inn, and that somewhere along the way I went from thinking about getting a more suitable long-distance bike to actually resolving to do so.

---

Next morning, after a glorious night's sleep in my very large bed in my very English room, I woke to a methodical on-again-off-again clanking sound. Five or six steady clanks, then 15 seconds of silence, then five or six steady clanks, then silence, then the clanks again. It was, it turned out, a tent crew; specifically, it was a beefy young man with a sledge hammer, driving stakes for the giant white tent that had already been unrolled and placed on the inn's back lawn. Ah, yes, I remembered, it's somebody's wedding day—and time for me to stow my bags and bike on the boat and head around to the other side the island. After coffee and scones again on the porch—this time the back porch so I could watch them finish putting up the tent (it's remarkable how fast they do it)—I did just that.

Soon I was heading down Thompson Creek, then Cox Creek, and into Eastern Bay. Today's mission: around Bloody Point and up the west side of the island to the Bay Bridge marina, then hop on the bike again and check out the South Island Trail. Just thinking about it made my tuckus throb a bit, but I was determined to finish what I'd started.

Finding my way to E dock at the Bay Bridge Marina, was a snap, compared to Thursday's adventure. There was no chance of overshooting it, for starters, because . . . well, because I simply couldn't go much farther. Slip E-14 was just about as far into the northeast corner of the marina as one could get—a convenient spot indeed, in terms of proximity to both the showers and the road leading out of the marina. Later this evening, I would very much appreciate those things; the showers perhaps most of all.

The previous day's ride, by my low-tech reckoning, had been 10 or 12 miles. This afternoon's ride, to Romancoke and back, would be more like 16 miles. And, it turned out, 16 far less interesting miles than those of the Cross Island Trail. The trail begins in earnest at Matapeake State Park—much of which, until 1952 had been the Kent Island terminal of the long-running Matapeake–Sandy Point Ferry, made obsolete that same year by the spanking-new Chesapeake Bay Bridge. The site is now shared by the Maryland Marine Police Academy and the state park—which is in fact leased by Queen Anne's County and comprises a strip of sandy beach, a fishing pier and the renovated the ferry terminal building, now called the Matapeake Clubhouse. The park grounds hold yet another fascinating study in obsolescence: the vast and spooky remains of what must be the largest failure (speaking only literally) of Bay environmental research: the Chesapeake Bay Hydraulic Model. Built in the 1970s, this enormous concrete scale model of the Chesapeake never had a chance to prove itself; because of advances in computer modeling, it was obsolete before it was even finished. And all that remains of the sprawling site is the massive steel shed, nearly 300 yards long, that was built to house it, and the nearly mile-long road around it, now being reclaimed by weeds and scrub.

All this, I'm sorry to report, turned out to be the most interesting part of the South Island Trail experience. Perhaps I'm being unfair. Perhaps my opinion is more than a little colored by pain. Perhaps you shouldn't trust the word of someone who that day decided to name is bicycle Golgotha—a word that comes from the hill in Jerusalem where Christ was crucified, a word that is now a common noun meaning "place of great suffering, torment or martyrdom." I won't go so far as to call myself a martyr, but oh there was suffering and torment that day. And that may have something to do with my dim view of the South Island Trail. That, and how enjoyable can a bike trail be if it's never more than 50 feet from a very busy 50-mph road?

Oh, and one more thing: How enjoyable can a bike trail be if, for many long stretches of it, there are stop signs every 100 feet or so telling bikers not only to stop, but to dismount? Seriously. Under the stop sign it says BIKERS DISMOUNT. The Cross Island Trail also had some of these obnoxious signs, but not nearly as many as the southern trail—where they marked not only every crossroad but every driveway. There had to be fifty of them. A simple YIELD I could live with, or CAUTION, or even BE VERY, VERY CAREFUL CROSSING THIS DRIVEWAY . . . but dismount? No, call me a scofflaw, but that's just silly. A road, yes; a driveway, no.

*A woodsy bit of the South Island Trail, which parallels Route 8 from Matapeake to Romancoke.*

So, given all that, is it any wonder I was muttering blue oaths under my breath for pretty much the entire eight-mile return trip, from Romancoke to the marina—a trip that, somehow, was just as predominantly uphill as it had been in the opposite direction?

Or that I slept the sleep of the righteous, and the half-dead, that night in the Albin's V-berth? Or that I was happy to stand at the helm all the way across the Bay the next day, back to Back Creek? Or that within a week I'd become the proud owner of a much lighter, much more distance-friendly bicycle?

Oh, and how much for those padded shorts, sir?

---

This article first appeared in *Chesapeake Bay Magazine* in September 2011. Author T. F. Sayles is editor of the magazine.

*Annapolis:*

# **West Side Story**

**8**

*The thriving neighborhood of West Annapolis, just a short walk from peaceful Weems Creek, offers boaters a distinct and practical alternative to the busy harbor and streets of downtown Annapolis.*

*by Wendy Mitman Clarke*

Growing up on Weems Creek in Annapolis, Stan Wood knew all about the swimming, sailing and crabbing in summer, and the ice-skating and sledding in winter. Even then, as a busy, easily distracted youngster, he knew it was a special place. But as an adult—and the owner of a 44-foot catamaran—Wood these days is seeing the creek, and the community of West Annapolis along its southeastern side, from a broader perspective. And it keeps getting better.

Wood and his wife and three kids returned to Weems Creek this summer after a year of cruising in the Bahamas. His mother still lives here, and he planned to use her place as home base until they could move back into their home in Severna Park. "We knew we could leave the boat on a mooring and have a relatively secure place to leave it briefly if we had to," he says. "But having been cruising for a year, the first thing that jumped out at us was that it was a really great place to come into Annapolis and get everything you need, and it's all easy to get to on foot."

Though he'd lived here most of his life, Wood had just learned what savvy cruisers have known all along; Weems Creek and West Annapolis are two of the best-kept secrets on Maryland's Severn River. While its bigger sister just around the corner gets all the attention—as well as the crowds and traffic—West Annapolis is like a small town within a town, compact, pretty, un-touristy and neighborly. For boaters it has the added bonus of something that downtown Annapolis, despite its historic cachet and gourmet ice-cream parlors, profoundly lacks: basic necessities like a grocery store, laundry, and even doctors and dentists—not to mention a couple of day-spas, beauty salons and excellent dining. And it's all within walking distance from the public landing where you can beach your dinghy. If you still feel a burning need to visit downtown Annapolis, that's easy enough to do by taxi or on the free Annapolis transit bus you can flag down as it passes through West Annapolis. (If you're up for a brisk walk, it's only about two flat miles.) And when you're done, you can head back to the quietude of Weems Creek, where it's still possible to see bald eagles and otters, go for a clarifying swim, and catch a perch or two for breakfast.

This month West Annapolis will hold its 15th annual Oktoberfest (on October 2). Its main drag, Annapolis Street, will be closed to vehicular traffic so the shopkeepers can bring tables of their wares onto the street and locals can listen to the oom-pah band, watch the parade, peruse the community's varied shops (everything from antiques to clocks to British culinary imports) and nosh some of the wurst, schnitzel, hot German potato salad and melt-in-your-mouth sauerkraut that Regina's Restaurant is known for.

When I first learned about Oktoberfest (just this summer) a little voice in my head said, "Duh." I have noodled around Weems Creek for 15 years in every season in a variety of boats—paddled to its headwaters in a kayak, jumped in for many a swim off our sailboat, sped around its mouth in a Laser on a blustery early fall day, even raced radio-controlled model America's Cup yachts on its well protected coves. I've known it as a waterway severely threatened by overdevelopment and defended by a cadre of fierce loyalists, as well as a quiet, hole-in-the-wall kind of gathering place for cruising boaters from all over the world who are traveling north or south through the Bay and along the East Coast. It's been a part of my life ever since I came to Annapolis, and for the last year-and-a-half, it's been my home.

Yet, just like Stan Wood, only recently did I realize my perspective has been lacking. Though I had been a regular customer of Art Things, a cornerstone business here and one of the niftiest art supply stores in the area, I hadn't really paid attention to West Annapolis as its own entity, nor had I linked it closely enough with Weems Creek. Sometimes it's hard to see what's right in your own backyard, but that's no excuse. A small journey was in order.

---

As early as the 1650s, people figured out this was a fine spot. In 1658, John Norwood, the sheriff of what was then known as Providence County (now called Anne Arundel County) patented 230 acres along Weems Creek, much of which is the peninsula that stretches along the creek's southeastern side and faces the Severn River to the northeast. Over the generations it passed through various hands, mostly being farmed, but by 1868 there was debt owed, so the land went to public auction. The notice of auction published in the local newspaper—appropriately lavish in description as these sorts of things are, even today—made it sound like a patch of Eden, which it probably almost was:

> The soil is of fine quality, producing all the county crops, and [is] particularly adapted to the growth of early fruits and vegetables. The site is one of the most beautiful on the Severn, command-ing an extensive view of the grounds of the Naval Academy and

*Retropolitan antiques shop is one of several along Annapolis Street in West Annapolis. Preced-ing pages: A West Annapolis Shopping District sign outside a clothing consignment store.*

across the channel. It is distant less than a mile from Annapolis by a good road. On the farm are good landings for shipping and the railroad is within half a mile. The improvements consist of a small dwelling, two fine barns, servants quarters, corn house and all the necessary buildings.

---

Luther Giddings, a major of the First Ohio Volunteers who served in the Mexican War, bought the 237 acres for $46 an acre, and in 1884 he divided it between his daughters Elizabeth and Catherine. Six years later, the Maryland General Assembly incorporated the area, and the Giddings sisters chose lawyer George Melvin (who also owned, with William Ridgely, the *Maryland Republican* newspaper and eventually became president of Annapolis Banking and Trust) to develop a planned residential community. It would have ample gardens and even oyster farming, since the state let residents stake off up to five acres of creek or river bottom to cultivate the bivalves.

According to a 1963 newspaper story in the Annapolis *Evening Capital*, Elizabeth Giddings had named her part of the land—on the tip of the peninsula, facing the Severn and running along part of Weems Creek—Wardour, after the English castle and estate where Anne Arundell spent her childhood. True to its namesake, Wardour was destined to become an exclusive neighborhood and remains so today, its homes nestled among enormous old trees along narrow, winding lanes reminiscent of the dirt paths that once carried residents to and fro.

West Annapolis, abutting Wardour to the southwest and lying farther upstream along Weems Creek, was also developing into a residential neighborhood, thanks to Melvin's enchanting vision, which was described in a promotional brochure published around 1890: "Nothing is lacking to complete rural comfort and enjoyment," the brochure said. With the Annapolis and Baltimore Short Line Railroad running across the Severn River at Wardour and stopping at a station in West Annapolis (about where the firehouse is now, near the corner of Taylor Avenue and Annapolis Street), it was a painless 50-minute train ride to Baltimore. Melvin encouraged businessmen to build their summer homes here and enjoy "the finest water views in Maryland" with "bracing breezes that add a health and charm and vigor of life that is sought for in vain in city homes or at points further inland." Lots were drawn at 50 by 150 feet and sold for $50 and up, cash or installment plan. With avenues carrying names like Giddings, Ridgely and Melvin, and a few businesses springing up to support the fledgling neighborhood, West Annapolis set down its roots and, by all accounts, thrived.

---

It's lunchtime on a warm summer afternoon, but sitting next to the beverage cooler at Annapolis Gourmet Deli at the corner of Melvin Avenue and Annapolis Street and savoring a delicious bowl of home-made split-pea soup with barley, I am pleasantly cool—even though the front door seems to be open more than closed, what with all the people coming and going. It's a three-block walk from the dinghy landing at the end of Tucker Street to the high-test coffee and tasty softball-size muffins served here, among other delectables.

Gus Leanos, who has owned this establishment for some 18 years, is holding court behind the deli counter, which is topped with baskets of fruit, bagels, Tootsie Rolls and rectangular plastic towers that dispense a variety of coffee beans. From behind the counter's glass, a plate of lemon squares calls my name. The walls are covered with photos, and a television in the corner, perched over the chips rack, keeps visitors apprised of the news and weather. Over my shoulder, on top of the beverage cooler, are stacks of books, among them the *History of Thoroughbred Racing in America,* the *20th Century Baseball Chronicle, Alistair Cook's America,* the *Random House Dictionary* and the *Sports Encyclopedia Baseball 2000.* My eye falls to a chalkboard menu and something called a Ziggy, for $2. I wonder out loud what that is.

"I think it's a bagel with onion and tomato or something," says a customer at the table next to me (there are only three tables inside, and a few outside on the sidewalk, under an awning). "You have to ask Gus. For all I know there are custom Ziggies."

Turns out he's not far wrong; a Ziggy is a cream cheese bagel with onion and tomato. And he's right about asking Gus, who serves pithy bits of information and history along with the bagels, muffins and Zig-gies between serving customers. Most neighborhoods have some kind of gathering spot, and this is the place in West Annapolis. Evidently, it has been for generations. Harold R. Parkinson, who has lived in the neigh-borhood since 1930, wrote a booklet of his memories of the community. Of what is now the Annapolis Gourmet Deli he writes that it was a small corner store when he was a boy. "The favorite of all the kids in the neighborhood was the candy case, if we had a few pennies. And if we didn't we would hunt soda bottles and return them to the store, two pennies for a small bottle and five pennies for a large soda bottle. With Mrs. Shawn behind the candy case, we would tell her that we wanted one of these, one of these and two of these . . . the corner store was a meeting place for the kids in the neighborhood."

These days the kids are much older, but between morning coffee and the lunchtime crowd you are bound to find locals, a cruising boater or two and even people who come from five miles across town to enjoy the food, the laid-back atmosphere and the ample street parking (no meters). And it's the obvious place to begin my exploration of West Annapolis's shopping district, located mostly along two long blocks of Annapolis Street. True, I had made a few forays into West Annapolis before, but I'd never simply strolled along, stopped wherever I felt like and talked with business owners.

"Parking, parking, parking, free parking," says Pris Foust, when I ask her what sets West Annapolis apart from Annapolis proper. "And not only parking but the friendliness . . . and there are no T-shirt shops here, definitely not, and I hope it never comes to that." Foust and I are sitting

*Boats at a home dock on Weems Creek.*

in her shop, Pris' Paper Parlor, which she has owned and operated for 27 years. Like many of the businesses in West Annapolis, it's located in what was once a residence, so when you walk up the steps onto the porch and inside, you feel an instant, subtle hominess. Foust started the business, she says, when she moved to Annapolis from McLean, Va., and was so unhappy she decided to throw a party. "I tried to find some invitations," she says, "but there was not an invitation I would send to my worst enemy." The town needed a good stationery shop, so she opened one. "There was another shop on the street, and that was Art Things. And there was Black-Eyed Susan. Those were the only two shops."

Interestingly, all three of these early shops were started by women, and even today, most West Annapolis businesses are female-owned. Another of the founders was Lydia Nolan, who began Art Things some 30 years ago and has since passed it on to her daughter Laurie. As a mom myself, with two rambunctious kids to entertain onboard, I can highly recommend the shop for its intelligent, fun and educational art supplies. Several times a year I make a pilgrimage to Art Things to supply the boat with creative stuff that will keep the kids happy for hours. The shop sits on the edge of West Annapolis, right next to the remains of the old Annapolis and Baltimore Short Line rail bed, hidden in the thick trees and greenery.

Laurie Nolan, like the other shopkeepers, says that most of her business comes from locals. "We don't strive to get tourists here, but we welcome them," she tells me. "I think we're always striving for recognition. We're always struggling to have an established identity as a viable shopping district with lots of services. These are all individual-owned businesses. There are no Banana Republics, no Starbucks."

"I think most of the people who have shops on this street are pretty independent people, which makes it good and bad, you know," says Nelson Stammer, a clock maker who owns Clocks Classics and Collectibles, where he repairs and sells all manner of timepieces, chronometers, barometers and even music boxes. Amid the melodic ticking, gonging and chiming inside his shop, I fall for several of his extraordinary antique clocks and an 1850 symphonium music box with a burled walnut case that plays a tinkling version of the "Wedding March."

Foust says she has customers who have been coming to her Paper Parlor for 25 years, and she's not surprised that West Annapolis has, over the years, consistently drawn in new businesses. Shops like hers, that have anchored the community for decades, help the roots stay strong. "Gus has been here forever, Regina [of Regina's Restaurant] has been here eighteen years. Tiger's Eye [a jewelry shop] has been here about fifteen years," she says. It's much less expensive to buy or rent a building here, she says, and since it's literally a minute to Route 50 and all points west and east, it's far more convenient than traveling downtown and fighting the Annapolis parking monster.

It's also easy to get around. The heart of the commercial business district is about six blocks (it includes several blocks of professional offices), with most of the shops along Annapolis Street. "It's an afternoon of walking around," says Laurie Nolan. "It's not overwhelming." Indeed, in a day's cruise of West Annapolis a visiting boater can choose between Regina's and Annapolis Gourmet Deli for breakfast and lunch, or stop at Great Harvest Bread Co. for muffins, fresh breads and cookies. For dinner, there is Northwoods, a well established restaurant known for its consistently fine cuisine. Between all this eating, you can take your pick of antiques and consignment shops, a variety of salons, a holistic healing center offering massage, acupuncture and yoga, shop for the perfect baby gift at the Giant Peach (another longtime business here), find beautiful wind chimes, garden ornaments and all things avian at the Wild Bird Center, get your grocery shopping done at Graul's Market and score a nice bottle of wine at the Rite Aid next door. After all that, it's a short walk down Tucker Street to the local launch ramp, where you hop in your dinghy and head out into the creek, without which the story of West Annapolis would only be half told.

———————

It's late winter—the ospreys aren't even here yet—but the day is unseasonably warm, and I am exploring Weems Creek by kayak. Like the community beside it, the creek is a comfortable size, not too big, not too small. It's just a mile or so from its mouth (at what's known as Priest Point) to its headwaters near the thundering lanes of Route 50, remaining quite wide and deep most of the way, then slowly narrowing and shallowing. I paddle past the triangular white moorings that dot the first half-mile of the creek. When a hurricane threatens the Bay, the U.S. Naval Academy brings its deep-draft sailboats to these moorings to ride out the weather. At all other times they're first-come-first-served for boaters who want to hang off a ball for an evening or spend an afternoon swimming.

Hugging the north side of the creek, I skim past expansive waterfront manses, many with docks, until I pass beneath the Weems Creek draw-bridge, a swing span that carries two lanes of traffic on Ridgely Avenue and was recently rebuilt. Not far beyond that is the towering fixed bridge that carries four noisy lanes of Rowe Boulevard—the main drag into Annapolis. A new bridge is being built alongside the crumbling old one, and its tall gray pillars and arches are a handsome improvement from the dirty brown concrete and exposed rebar beneath the older bridge.

I pass beneath the bridges and head toward a long stretch of un-developed land on the creek's northwest side, where the creek starts to narrow and shallow, and the deep woods shelter songbirds and turtles, hawks and blue herons. It's an incongruous spot; another five minutes of paddling and I'd be a stone's throw from Route 50—and nearly as close to the sprawling infrastructure of the county detention center, the Anne Arundel Medical Center and a huge shopping mall. The incessant drum-ming of vehicles on Rowe Boulevard and the highway never quite dis-sipates (except in a heavy snow, when a cottony, blissful silence falls over the creek), but the depth of these woods and the small hills and valleys mute the noise. I pull up to a strip of copper-colored beach, exposed by the low tide, and find a handful of perfectly smooth orange stones that

*Shops in West Annapolis's shopping district, lined with sunflowers and black-eyed susans.*

have leached over time from the bank. I know a hawk is passing overhead because I see its shadow reflecting on the water beside me. Here in the lee of the slight northwest breeze, the sun is warm on my face. Across the creek houses perch on the high hills, and docks poke out into the water, but along this small stretch of woods all is as it has been for generations.

This is the Hock property, 16.7 acres of land that the State Highway Administration for decades planned to develop. Several years ago, the SHA agreed to place these acres into an environmental trust—a monumental victory for the Weems Creek Conservancy, which has fought like a tiger for the creek's health and welfare since the mid-1960s, when the SHA started clearing land to build Route 50, and again several years ago when the heavily traveled road was widened. "The Hock property at the head of the creek was slated for all kinds of crazy stuff," says Elizabeth McWethy, arguably the conservancy's matriarch and a lifelong resident of Weems Creek who remembers when the noisiest things around here were the cicadas in summer and the clip-clopping of horses on Ridgely Avenue. "It is seventeen acres between Route 50 and the creek, and it is vital."

Any creek surrounded by dense development is threatened, but Weems Creek's problems are compounded by the acres of parking lots

*Sailboats on mooring balls in quiet Weems Creek.*

(to serve the mall and hospital, for instance) and Route 50, impervious surfaces that send tons of tainted stormwater runoff into the creek. After an especially hard or long rain, the plume of mud and sediment often reaches nearly to the creek's mouth, and its upper reaches have steadily shallowed over the years. In mid-July, a broken pump at a sewage substation dumped 10,000 gallons of wastewater and sewage into the creek, prompting health officials to close part of it temporarily.

McWethy and the band of residents that formed the conservancy have consistently and stubbornly defended the creek over the years. McWethy, who famously threatened to strip naked and tie herself to a tree when the SHA started widening Route 50, remembers a creek rich with grasses, fish, crabs and oysters. "I guess you could say the creek brought me up. My experience of it is different than most of the people on it today," she says. "People should imagine what it would be like without it."

I push the kayak off the beach and head back toward the creek's deep water which remains remarkably clear much of the time, despite the troubles upstream. As I pass the foot of Tucker Street, I toy with the idea of beaching the kayak and walking up to Gus's for a muffin and a cup of coffee. But out over the creek a hawk is soaring up in the blue, and so I just keep going.

---

This article first appeared in *Chesapeake Bay Magazine* in October 2005. Wendy Mitman Clarke was then executive editor of the magazine and is now an editor-at-large and a frequent contributor.

*St. Michaels:*

## 9

### Nobody Doesn't Like St. Mikes

*Whether you've been there once or a dozen times, St. Michaels is the kind of place you just keep going back to. Why? Because you never have the same visit twice.*

*by Ann Levelle*

One hundred degree heat and nearly 100 percent humidity was not going to keep the crowds away from the Chesapeake Bay Maritime Musuem during its annual Antique and Classic Boat Show. Know why? First, the museum is packed to its figurative gills with jaw-droppingly stunning classic boats. Second, this is St. Michaels—Chesapeake country's favorite destination—the town you keep going back to, no matter how many times you've been before. Case in point: My husband John and I, along with our friends Drew and Kinley Bray. The four of us had decided to come down to St. Michaels on the Saturday of last year's show since none of us had been there in ages, so this seemed like a perfect excuse for the adventure. And aside from the heat, it was. But that's the beauty of St. Michaels, really, heat seems to have no bearing on anyone's good times in this summer tourist haven. Both boaters and landlubbers alike find its charms irresistible despite what nature throws at them.

We wandered the museum grounds gazing longingly at all the lustrous wooden Chris-Crafts, Trumpys and Matthews on the hard and in the water. Every one of the boats—from tiny runabouts to 50-foot wooden yachts—has been painstakingly restored, woodwork gleaming from God only knows how many coats of varnish. We also strolled through the vendor area for a bit, grazing among the artwork, crafts and throngs of cool old boat parts and accessories. By the time we'd done the rounds of the show, we were all hot and hungry and were ready to go next door to the Crab Claw for a little lunch. We got a table in the blissfully cold dining room surprisingly fast, considering the crowd. Then we dined on a couple of baskets of clam strips and a dozen crabs for good measure. They were fantastic as always.

As we were walking back to the car, my cell phone rang: It was my old pal Annie calling from South Carolina.

"Hey, whatcha doing?"

"I'm down in St. Michaels, we went out for crabs and to the antique boat festival."

"Sounds like fun! Where's St. Michaels?" she asked (I swear I'm not making this up).

"Seriously? You grew up in Maryland and don't know where St. Michaels is?"

"Um . . . guess not. So where is it and what's there?"

"Well, it's on the Eastern Shore," I replied. "And it's a cool little boating town with lots of good restaurants and a huge maritime museum. It's a pretty fun place."

"Oh," she said, sounding excited. "You want to take me there when I come up this week? We need to get a boat trip in when I visit, you know."

"Done," I said, "We'll take a powerboat too, so we don't have to waste precious time sailing down."

---

Fast forward to Tuesday, *another* record-breaking hot and humid June day. The sky and water were an equally hazy blue-gray color, and the water was as flat as could be. I couldn't be happier to be zooming down the Bay in one of the Chesapeake Boating Club's Albin 28s with the wind in my hair. Annie was pretty excited too, since our last few outings had been during similar weather, but slinking along at five knots in a sailboat. In the Albin, though, we made it from Annapolis to St. Michaels in a delightfully short two hours, and were quite surprised when we rounded red "4" to find an enormous cruise ship docked at the maritime museum. We slowed to the requisite five knots and puttered toward town, admiring the Hooper Strait Lighthouse as we neared the museum. As cruise director, I also thought it prudent to swing through Fogg Cove to show Annie the Inn at Perry Cabin, where a good bit of the movie *Wedding Crashers* was shot. She was duly impressed, especially by the movie part.

Back in the harbor we aimed for the telltale red roofs of St. Michaels Marina. The marina's tall flag staffs, bearing both Old Glory and the Union Jack were also visible between some of the larger boats docked at the fuel dock. Fortunately for me (lacking confidence in docking as I do), St. Michaels Marina has a lot of very big slips to accommodate the Bay's finest. So I had no trouble sliding the comparatively tiny Albin 28 into the basin and then to the spacious slip—and, equally important, to the awaiting friendly and very helpful dockhand.

Anxious to get into town for some lunch, we kept things brief at the marina office and store. There we met owner Mike Morgan, who personally gave us a quick rundown on the marina, the WiFi, the pool, shower combos, etc.—and, perhaps hearing our stomachs growl, the lowdown on the three restaurants that surround the marina: St. Michaels Crab & Steak House, Town Dock Restaurant and Foxy's Marina Bar. And the mix of Old Glory and the Union Jack? What's that about? I asked. Ah, he said,

*Small boats line the pathway along the water to the Crab Claw and Chesapeake Bay Maritime Museum. Preceding pages: Hooper Strait Lighthouse standing sentinel at the Chesapeake Bay Maritime Museum.*

that's a nod to the persistent old (and highly dubious) historical meme about St. Michaels, "the town that fooled the British" during the War of 1812.

Of course, Annie, who didn't even know where St. Michaels was, had no idea what he was talking about. So, as we began our short walk to town—all two blocks up Mulberry Street, that is—I expanded on Morgan's explanation, telling her that during the War of 1812 the British were poised to attack St. Michaels—which was a target because of its dozen or so shipbuilding facilities. The townspeople, in addition to chaining off the harbor entrance, lit lanterns in the trees far behind the actual town, causing the British gun ships to overshoot the town. The trouble with this legend, I told Annie, was that the actual attack happened well after dawn, which seriously undermines the whole lantern story. Not to mention that at least one house—that one in fact, I said, pointing to the so-called Cannonball House that we'd just passed on Mulberry Street—was actually hit and still has burn marks from the cannonball rolling down the stairs. (As it turned out, the Cannonball House was now up for sale, too . . . for a whopping $1,495,000. Later I found out that the house, built in 1805, sold in 1831 for $1,000. Ahh, inflation.)

Annie wasn't exactly riveted by my brief history lesson—which was good, because not only had we reached St. Michaels' main drag, Talbot Street, but also, I was fresh out of history. For the moment, anyway. Since it was a Tuesday, the red brick sidewalks were pretty empty, but as we walked along, peering into shop windows, we saw quite a few browsers indoors. We had no trouble getting a table at the tiny Key Lime Cafe, a bright and airy restaurant with a very welcoming staff, housed in a tiny old cottage on Talbot Street. The menu, which changes regularly with the seasons and at the whim of the chef, was limited, featuring just a few appetizers, sandwiches and salads, but we each found something tasty. Honestly though, we'd have been quite happy with nothing but ice water, because it was furiously hot outside. Thankfully our waitress was excellent in her refilling duties and we had a couple of nice salads to hold us over for our afternoon of sightseeing.

After lunch we continued north on Talbot toward the maritime museum. Annie, obviously had never been there, and I, despite having visited the previous weekend, was more than happy to visit again since over the weekend I had focused solely on antique boats. Just inside the museum gate, docent Rick Green met us to give us the rundown of the marina exhibits. Volunteer docents are an important part of the Chesapeake Bay Maritime Museum experience, and Green was one of many enthusiastic guides we'd have throughout the day.

We started our tour at the boatbuilding shed, where four shipwrights were hard at work on various wooden boats—a lapstrake skiff, an Adirondack fishing canoe and a duck canoe.

Volunteer docent Mary Sue Traynelis led us through the shop, explaining various planking methods to us (namely lapstrake vs. board-on-board). Then she showed us the painting room, while she explained the Apprentice For a Day program, in which anyone (kids, teens, whole families) can spend the day helping shipwrights build replicas of Bay boats—from Smith Island skiffs to canoes. Volunteers can choose to work for a single day, a weekend or any number of days throughout the 17-week boatbuilding process. She ushered us to one of the boats they had just finished building, which took a little more than 18 weeks to finish (due to lack of apprentices).

We bade Mary Sue good-bye and continued our tour around the museum grounds, visiting the lighthouse—and of course every air-conditioned exhibit we could find: the At Play on the Bay history exhibit, an art exhibit featuring watercolor master Marc Castelli, and a Holland Island history exhibit. We also managed to at least peer into the outdoor boat shed, the oystering building and the Waterman's Wharf, where you can try your hand at oyster tonging, eeling and catching crabs in a tank.

After a couple of hours, we figured we'd done our scholarly tourist duty at the museum and had earned ourselves a little time either with a frosty beverage or at the marina pool (or both). We didn't get halfway back to the marina, though, before a frosty beverage found us. A teen-age girl was handing out coupons to the Drink Shack, or, as the cutely painted sign on the sidewalk read, DRINK SHACK IN DA BACK. She pointed us between two gift shops to a tiny oasis where a man in a brightly painted building was selling fruit smoothies, fresh lemonade and virgin frozen pina coladas and daiquiris. Tiki umbrellas and tables were set up atop sand colored gravel and we enjoyed a couple of fresh smoothies in the shade—a true oasis on this hot and humid afternoon. We finished our beverages on the way back to the marina, where the small pool, nestled between the docks and the marina office/ship's store beckoned.

"So what do you think of St. Michaels?" I asked Annie as we lingered neck deep in the blissfully cold water.

"It's nice! I didn't expect there'd be this much to do in a tiny Eastern Shore town. I'm not sure we'll be able to cover it all in two days."

My sentiments exactly. It had been a few years since I'd spent any extended time in town, and I'd forgotten how much there is to do here. At the risk of sounding like a tourist brochure (which, by the way if you need any, there's a tiny shack just south of the maritime museum entrance on Talbot Street that has hundreds of them available for the taking, including town maps and brochures on just about every attraction in town), St. Michaels really does have a bit of something for everyone. Boaters get some great marinas or a nice anchorage with only a short dinghy ride to town. And whether you come by land or sea, you get a world-class maritime museum—which is to say, all the Chesapeake history and culture you could want—plus tons of restaurants and shopping, a couple of excellent hotels, B&Bs galore, boating excursions and tours, and a dash of history. In case that wasn't enough, the town hosts a ton of town-wide events throughout the year that draw thousands of visitors to each—log canoe races, summer concert series, a fall festival, Christmas in St. Michaels, boat festivals and rendezvous, the list keeps on going. And with every visit you feel a little more a part of the tiny community

*A sailboat at anchor in Fogg Cove in front of the maritime museum's crab shack and oystering exhibit buildings.*

that ties it all together.

Phew, okay brochure rant over. It was six in the evening and the day's heat finally started to let up. Annie and I waited until the bells at nearby Christ Church ended their evening concert, then headed back to the boat to clean up for dinner. We decided—wisely I might add—to eat at Town Dock restaurant, which backs up to the marina, since hefty storms were predicted and we wanted to leave the boat open as long as possible. The restaurant, which touts itself as casual fine dining, has outdoor patio tables, but given the heat and upcoming storms, we opted to dine on the indoor patio, which boasts huge windows and a great view of the marina and the harbor.

Annie ordered excellent Panko fried oysters for an appetizer. By the time she (okay, we) finished these oh-so-plump oysters, we could hear the thunder rumbling in the distance. And about halfway through our dinners—shrimp scampi for Annie, and a delicious vegetable ravioli with a walnut cream pesto sauce for me—the increasing racket told us it was time to dash to the boat and button things up, so we could finish our dinner without worry. It was a heck of a storm and we sat for a good hour and drank our bottle of sauvignon blanc and watched the show.

---

The next morning proved just as hot as the last, but not to worry—we had a day of mostly air-conditioned activities planned. We started out the day as I have started nearly every other day in St. Michaels—at Carpenter Street Saloon for breakfast. It's a no frills kind of place, but provides the kind of perfectly tasty and inexpensive breakfast that cures most any over-drinking issues and sets you up for a good day of sightseeing. And clearly it's *the* place to be in the morning, as the breakfast crowd was pretty decent even on a Wednesday.

We filled up on egg sandwiches and scrapple and such, then moved over to the saloon side of Carpenter Street to watch the U.S./Slovenia World Cup match on TV. For a good while it was just us and the bartender, but as the morning progressed, it became clear that tourists aren't the only clientele here at C-Street. By halftime in the game, the bar was hopping with local servers and bartenders from other restaurants who were all hanging out eating and gossiping (presumably before their lunch shifts started). Since we had a captive audience of locals at our service, we asked what we should do while we were in St. Mikes. Somewhat confused by the question, they only offered one reasonably straight answer: eat and drink. Then they mentioned the winery and brewery were both fun outings.

After the soccer match had ended we were ready to hit the town. Annie had insisted at some point during our visit we should eat crabs, so I decided now was the time, and off we went to the obvious place: the Crab Claw, the town's biggest crabhouse and arguably the most well known and popular on the entire Bay. Since we'd had a pretty hearty breakfast, we opted to order crabs by the piece (at a pretty good deal: $3 per crab), hush puppies and a pitcher of water. We happily picked our extra sweet and delicious half-dozen crabs on the covered patio while watching boats come and go in the harbor. It's the quietest I've ever seen the Crab Claw, I told Annie, noting that weekend nights the joint is all but throbbing, with people packed in like sardines. When our check came, I'd realized I'd made a classic rookie mistake—I'd forgotten to go to the ATM before lunch. Everyone who has ever been to St. Michaels and the Crab Claw knows that they don't take plastic here, and even though I'd been only four days before, it had totally slipped my mind. (Fortunately the restaurant has an ATM out front. I can only imagine the money that the owners of said machine make on fees.)

Next up on our list of obligatory St. Michaels to-dos: shopping. We strolled Talbot Street, going into each blessedly cool shop and spending way more time in each than we normally would have. Thanks to the heat, we went into some artsy-crafty stores that normally wouldn't have interested us. I was pleasantly surprised at how few stores carried the cheesy stuff—St. Mikes T-shirt and crab magnets and such. We had made our way down Talbot Street in about an hour or so, and since we're not big shoppers, that had been ample time to browse. Now we had arrived at something a little more to our liking—the St. Michaels Winery.

We found the sign for the winery on the southern end of Talbot Street, and walked the block down Marengo Street to the tasting room, which is housed in the town's old mill complex. After we'd found a seat at one of several large round tables (perched atop old wine barrels), our pourer/server handed us menus and explained how their tasting system worked. You can pick wines a la carte or choose a "flight" of wines that the winery recommends you taste together. We chose the "staff favorites" flight, which included the winery's award-winners, dry whites and a couple of reds. The award-winnning Long Splice (delightfully dry and crisp), the pinot noir (smooth and creamy) and the Maryland Merlot (which tasted nothing like California merlots I've had) were my favorites. We also were able to taste a few all-Maryland wines, the grapes for which are grown at the winery's vineyard in nearby Wye Oak, Md., and the Martha Chambourcin, named after the *Martha Lewis*, which brings its varietals' grapes from a vineyard in Havre de Grace to St. Michaels each season. The winery, which opened in 2005, grows grapes at two Maryland locations, and buys from other Maryland growers.

After we finished off our wines, our very wine-literate servers packaged up our take-home souvenir wine glasses for us, and soon we were off for our next adventure: Eastern Shore Brewing! The brewery, which is just up Talbot Street from the winery, opened just two years ago but has already made a name for itself in the state. Three of their beers won medals in the Maryland Governor's Cup competition last October.

We sat at the bar of the sparsely decorated tasting room at the brewery and were met by a very tall, gregarious bartender with wild, dark curly hair and tattooed arms. I never got his name, but he immediately made us feel welcome. We ordered the flight of the day, which included all five beers on tap for the day—the Lighthaus Ale, a cherry brew, the Magic Hefeweizen, the St. Michaels Ale and the Knot So Pale Ale. We

*A workboat heading into St. Michaels Harbor, with the marina at the St. Michaels Harbour Inn & Spa in the background.*

weren't particularly impressed by the first three, but the final two were fantastic brews. While we were sipping our beers, we chatted with the only other folks at the bar, who were coincidentally from Columbia, Md.—where Annie and I had both grown up. We also got a chance to meet the establishment's young brewmeister, a recent college grad who said they'd be brewing again the next day, and it would be another hot day at the office. The bartender translated for us. They only brew every few weeks, and the process is extremely hot. Also, you can tell when they're brewing because you can smell it throughout a several block radius (which is to say, all of St. Michaels).

Sufficiently buzzed from our wine and beer tasting adventures, we headed for the pool again. After an hour or so of lounging poolside we took showers and were ready to hit the town again. This time we were off to Ava's pizzeria and wine bar for dinner. We had been told by folks at Carpenter Street and the winery that Ava's had the best pizza in town, plus a great wine list and a ton of other good food. And right they all were.

Ava's occupies a classic St. Michaels home along Talbot Street, and the dining rooms are in the front two rooms of the house and on the front and back porches. The eat-in bar area is also in one of the main front

*Yachts lining the docks of St. Michaels Marina, with St. Michaels Crab & Steak House just beyond.*

rooms. It was immediately evident to us that this was where the locals eat. We saw and overheard a lot of local business conversations, the bartender obviously knew a lot of the customers by name, and nobody but Annie was sunburned.

We perused the extensive wine list, finally ordering a bottle of pinot noir to accompany our garlic mussels appetizer. Then we moved on to Ava's homemade pizza, choosing prosciutto, baby portobello mushrooms and spinach from the list of gourmet toppings. The pizza was fantastic, with a crispy, thin crust and perfectly bubbly cheese. Ava's makes everything in-house (including potato chips), using many local ingredients, and it definitely shined through.

While enjoying our great dinner, we discussed our trip. Annie liked St. Michaels, and agreed with the servers we had met at Carpenter Street that morning, that the best way to enjoy this town is to eat and drink. And we certainly had our fill of that. She also enjoyed the museum and crabhouse, which made her feel like she was at home in Chesapeake country.

And despite my having been here plenty of times, I was reminded why boaters are constantly flocking here and so many return multiple times in a summer: It's *comfortable* to come to St. Michaels. You always know what's in store for you, and the more you come back, the more it grows on you.

---

This article first appeared in *Chesapeake Bay Magazine* in February 2011. Ann Levelle is managing editor of the magazine.

*Easton:*

## Bike & Boat to Easton

**10**

*It's all the way up the Tred Avon River, but if you're okay in five feet of water and don't mind a one-mile walk or bike ride, the jolly old town of Easton can be your oyster.*

*by T. F. Sayles*

Here's an interesting coincidence: Easton, Md., that lovely old town on the Eastern Shore, seat of Maryland's Talbot County, was founded in 1710. And, as it turns out, that was also the year I first mentioned in an editorial planning session that Easton might actually be a decent boating destination, despite its apparent distance from the nearest deep water. The subject has come up in every planning session since 1710—and there have been several—and the conversation has always gone something like this:

*Me, pointing at the map:* "See, it's actually only a mile or so from downtown Easton to the Tred Avon River, which is definitely navigable this far up. So, if you could tie up there, or anchor out and find somewhere to leave a dinghy, it wouldn't be all that long a walk or bike ride into town."

*Someone else:* "Sure . . . you could do it in a powerboat, but not in a cruising sailboat, because you're down to four or five feet of water there. Also, that's a pretty small marina there and it's kind of an industrial spot, with fuel storage tanks all over the place. And to get into town from there you have to go through a pretty rough neighborhood. I wouldn't want to walk it at night." *Me:* "Hmm . . . Oh look, Oxford! We haven't done Oxford in a while, have we? . . ."

And so it would go, year after year, century after century—until last summer, when I was driving through Easton, on my way from Salisbury to Annapolis, and decided to scout out this theoretical boater's back door. I'm delighted to say I was right, because (a) it always delights me to be right, and (b) I now knew exactly where I'd be going on my upcoming and much anticipated September cruise: Easton. My spur-of-the-moment scouting trip revealed that, yes, the mile or so of Port Street that takes you from the river to downtown Easton is not exactly scenic. But it's not a "rough neighborhood" either, at least not in my vernacular. A bit down at the heels, yes. A modest-income neighborhood, yes. But rough? No. The scouting trip also revealed the funky but sublimely hospitable little camp store of a place that would be my beachhead for the trip—Easton Point Marina, which, according to owner and manager Kathy Meehan, did indeed have some open slips in early September and would be happy to reserve one for me. All that remained was to jigger my early-September schedule a bit, reserve one of the Chesapeake Boating Club's Albin 28s for, say, a Thursday through Saturday, and get my 15-speed Huffy out of the basement. The latter was important because my walking distance is limited these days, thanks to the ol' trick hip, which goes for only a quarter-mile or so before I start to toddle like Walter Brennan. (It's official, I'm old; not only do I have an arthritic hip, but my cultural references include Walter Brennan.) So I'd need a bike. But, on second thought, maybe I could rent one, which would save me a lot of bike-schlepping—lashing it to the car, lashing it to the boat, etc. Enter the Eastern Shore Bicycle Company, which was happy to rent me one of its very civilized and blessedly simple single-speed, coaster-brake, fat-tire Electra cruising bikes. The charge for three days was a reasonable $68, which included a helmet, a cable lock and, best of all, delivery to and pick-up from the spot of my choosing. Clever chap that I am, I chose the marina. Oh, and one more thing: I should book a room somewhere in town for at least one night of my stay. No, let's make it two nights. Yes, I know, that would be wasting a perfectly good V-berth . . . but what am I, an Explorer Scout? Yes, I could sleep on the boat all three nights. I could also dine every night on canned Vienna sausages from the Wawa, but I'm not going to do that either. No, given the choice, I'll go with mints on the pillow every time. The Tidewater Inn, with its $120 Labor Day special, was the hands-down winner of the price wars, so I booked it for Friday and Saturday nights. I'm a weenie, but I'm a frugal weenie.

And so it was that, after an uneventful three-hour cruise across the Bay, through Knapps Narrows, into the Choptank River and finally up the Tred Avon, I found my helmeted self pedaling eastward on Port Street, headed for dinner at Mason's Restaurant on Harrison Street— though not directly, because I had half an hour to kill before my seven o'clock reservation. I happily squandered the time exploring this pretty old town, learning the street names, relishing the perfectly temperate September air, and coming to a near-religious appreciation of the beauty and simplicity of a fixed-gear bicycle on flat land. Down Harrison Street, back up Washington Street, across on Dover, up Locust, down Harrison to South Lane and . . . oh, look, there's Mason's. And there's a bit of sturdy picket fence where I can chain the bike. Ah, how civilized I am, how light my carbon footprint on this fine summer evening.

Mason's, it turned out, was a very good place to start. What had begun in the 1960s as a small knickknack shop with its own line of chocolates gradually evolved over the years into a popular lunch spot. Now, after two significant expansions in the last decade, it has blossomed into one of

*A fanciful wall, tiles hand-painted by local grade-schoolers in the town's Idlewild Park.*
*Preceding pages: A view of Washington Street from alongside the 1805 Thomas Neale House.*

Talbot County's best restaurants—still with its own line of chocolates, and a lovely new coffee bar to boot. And chicken piccata to die for. That's what I ordered, though it's a miracle I had room for it after the "ciabatta tower" appetizer—a little orgy of toasted ciabatta bread and Gorgonzola. Add a glass of pinot grigio to that and you had one happy little scout riding his retro red-and-white bicycle back to the boat, whistling the theme song to "Leave It To Beaver" and having a good laugh at the nickname I'd come up with for the bike: Mrs. Cleaver. I know, it's not that funny. But to me, that night, under the influence of Gorgonzola, it was hilarious.

---

I had a lot on the agenda for the next day, so I resolved to get up at . . . nine-thirty? How did that happen? Oh well, up and at 'em at the crack of nine-thirty, then. I found Mrs. Cleaver exactly where I'd left her, chained to a post behind the marina building (egads, that doesn't sound right), and off we went, straight up Port Street. This is a quiet stretch of road nowadays, but it was designed to be just the opposite. Straight as a string, it was laid out in 1711, only a year after the town—originally named Talbot Courthouse—was established by the Colonial General Assembly. As it does now, the road led from Easton Point (once called either Cow's Landing or Cowe's Landing) to Washington Street just south of the courthouse, and it was of course the town's very lifeline. Easton Point was "the wharf," where the schooners and clippers and steamships came and went, where the lumber and lampshades came ashore and the oysters and canned tomatoes went aboard, and abroad.

So, with all that history passing under my wheels, it was appropriate that my first stop that morning would be the Historic Society of Talbot County's (HSTC) Museum and Gardens on Washington Street, to see about signing up for the weekly tour (Fridays at 11:30) of the restored 1810 James Neall House next door. But—my bad luck—only moments before I arrived the volunteer docent who normally does the Neall House tours had called to say he had a family emergency and wouldn't be coming in. Sorry, said the museum volunteer. Rats, said I. Maybe some other Friday. So I grabbed a self-guided tour map and struck out on my own, vowing to come back to the museum later that day to have a closer look at what looked like an intriguing exhibit on Talbot County during World War II.

As with so many towns of its age, fire has rewritten much of Easton's architectural history, erasing most of the wood-frame structures of the early 18th-century chapters and replacing them with the less vulnerable brick buildings of the Federal period (the Market Place Fire of 1878 must have been a big one; it's mentioned repeatedly in the self-guided tour). But that's not to say it's all brick or Victorian-era wood. Indeed, way down Washington Street, past the hospital and nearly out of the city proper, is what is thought to be the oldest frame building in all of Maryland: the 1684 Third Haven Meeting House, still used by the local Quaker community. And in the center of town there are a number of late 18th-century frame houses still standing—the 1789 Mary Jenkins House on Washington Street, for example, home of the HSTC's own revenue-generating consignment store, Tharpe Antiques.

After tooling around town for an hour or so, I began to see that everything I needed or wanted to see in Easton was in, or within easy walking distance of, what I came to think of as the Historic Rectangle—the four or five parallel blocks of Harrison and Washington streets between Goldsborough and South streets. That included the HSTC museum and historic properties, a dozen restaurants, three or four bars, at least four B&Bs, countless shops and galleries, the Avalon Theatre (where I planned to see a jazz trio on Saturday night), the Academy Art Museum (which a friend had told me not to miss and was on the next day's itinerary) and of course the Tidewater Inn.

I stopped for a late-breakfast nosh at the Coffee Cat, a sunny little corner cafe at the foot of Goldsborough Street, which had been known as Coffee East until late 2008. Now, under new management, it's the daytime half of a very popular commercial duet. Right next door is the Night Cat—a 60-seat nightclub that features local and regional music three or four nights a week, depending on the season. That night's act didn't ring a bell, but on the list of upcoming shows I saw more than a few names that did—Deanna Bogart, Tom Principato, Danni Rosner. Clearly not a musical backwater by any stretch.

Fortified with a breakfast sandwich and three cups of really good Guatemalan medium roast, I mounted Mrs. Cleaver again and. . . . Okay, I'm thinking maybe this whole Mrs. Cleaver thing isn't such a good idea. I think from here on I'll just go with "the bike." You'll know which bike I mean. There was only one. . . . So, anyway, I hopped on the bike and headed north on Washington Street, intent on visiting the HSTC Museum's World War II exhibit—before I realized that this would probably be my best chance to scoot out to the bike shop I'd looked up the night before—Easton Cycle and Sport—which, according to Mr. Google, was straight east from here on Goldsborough, out near Route 50. Mr. G was right, as he usually is, and I found the two things I was looking for at the bike shop: a rear-view mirror and some kind of hey-here-I-am-on-a-bike-please-don't-run-me-over flashing light or reflector strip. Twenty minutes later, with the help of a disposable hex wrench and my Swiss Army knife, I was all set—a side-view mirror attached to the left handlebar and a flashing light Velcro'd to my helmet. (I didn't realize it at the time, in the sunlight, but it was a damned powerful little light. I caught a glimpse of it that night in the reflection from a store window, and I looked like a channel marker on wheels. I imagined a boater groping his way up the Tred Avon two miles away: "Is that the red 16?" First mate: "No, it's some guy on a bicycle. He seems to be having fun.")

Anyway, safety issues resolved, I worked my way back west to the Historic Society Museum, eager to have a closer look at the World War II exhibit. I'm a sucker for World War II history, so it doesn't take much to get my attention . . . but this was really a fine exhibit. Taking up a good two-thirds of the museum's narrow but deep space, it was an intriguing glimpse of the war from the homefront, from the citizen's point of view, with most of the artifacts and photos donated by or on loan from Talbot countians: plane-spotting and civil defense, boatbuilding (Oxford Boat-yard built 126 boats and repaired 71), scrap-saving, sugar rationing, tire rationing (Price's Tire Shop switched to retreading and recapping for the duration), war bonds, victory gardens, blackout window shades, military uniforms, weapons, food packages for allied POWs, and, to my great surprise, a display about the German POW camp right here in Easton—from which, during the growing season, prisoners were sent out to work at local farms.

After a quick browse through the aforementioned Tharpe Antiques, across the street from the museum, I hopped back on the bike and rode a block south and then east to the Academy Art Museum at the corner of South and Harrison streets. I'm glad I listened to my friend and didn't miss this. It's a splendid old building, for starters, built just after the Civil War as the town's first public high school. Now its large, bare rooms and halls are filled with art—mostly photography during my visit, which coincided with an exhibit called *Picturing America, 1930–1960—Photographs from the Baltimore Museum of Art* (Walker

Evans, Dorothea Lange, Walter Rosenblum, et al.). Supplementing that was an exhibit featuring photographs from the museum's own collection, called *American Photographs from the 1950s Until Now*. It was all quite absorbing, as was the small (12-piece) but well chosen survey of paintings by Baltimore painter and academic Bennard Perlman.

Back out in the fresh air, strapping on the helmet once again, I was tempted to just head vaguely northeast and see what I might see, but good sense intervened, telling me it was time to move my base of operations from the boat to the Tidewater Inn. I pedaled back down Port Street, jammed two days worth of clothes into a backpack and locked up the boat. An hour later I was sprawled across the bed in my rather small room on the second floor of that lovely old 1949 hotel. But the term "small room" is relative, is it not? Indeed, to me, a six-foot man having spent the previous evening in a 5-foot-10-inch V-berth, this room seemed quite nearly cavernous. I took a shower, because I could. I took a nap, because I could.

Later, after a leisurely twilight ride around town (that's when I saw my flashing head reflected in the store window), I ventured only as far as the hotel's own restaurant for an excellent dinner of wood-grilled pork chops, accompanied by a warm apple and blue cheese slaw and marvelous, lemony German potatoes. Yet another splendid meal. Then it was off to bed, to that acre of mattress and embarrassment of pillows that awaited me in room 303. I drifted off to sleep, thinking how grand life would be if every day had such an easy, nourishing cadence: eat, ride the bike, absorb culture and/or history, ride the bike, eat,

*The restored Mary Jenkins House, ca. 1783, on Easton's South Washington Street. It is currently home to Tharpe Antiques & Decorative Arts.*

ride the bike, absorb culture and/or history, nap, eat, ride the bike, rinse, repeat. This I could get used to.

---

It all came to a lovely crescendo on the third day, and I use the musical term intentionally, because the day ended with a concert by jazz pianist Monty Alexander. That was at the Avalon Theatre, Easton's home-grown Art Deco movie theater from 1921 to 1985 and now its lively and very successful performing arts center. But I'm getting ahead of myself. The day—another perfect one, headed for the low 80s, with no discernible humidity—started with a tasty French toast breakfast at Darnell's Grill, a homey cafe next door to the Tidewater Inn, then a pleasantly aimless bike ride up and down the streets of the mostly residential neighborhood east of the historic rectangle.

Then I moseyed down to the north end of the rectangle, looking for the Saturday morning Farmer's Market I'd read about in one of the brochures I'd brought along to breakfast. The map had showed it at the north end of Harrison Street, just before it bends west and merges with Washington Street. And sure enough, that's where I found it. Actually I heard it before I saw it. That's the thing about bicycle touring; you hear things

*A ground-hugging sculpture in the town's 15-acre Idlewild Park.*

you'd never hear in a car. From a bike, a well attended farmer's market is audible from a block away. And this was well attended indeed. I didn't stay long though—not because there wasn't plenty to see and buy, but because there was no point in it. Whatever I bought here would have to survive transport by bike, boat and car, and that seemed like unnecessary vegetable cruelty to me.

So off I went for a bit more aimless exploring, then a light lunch (hummus and grilled naan) at the organically minded Out of the Fire restaurant on Goldsborough, and then back to the Tidewater Inn for a quiet afternoon of reading and people-watching from a rocker on the hotel's shady wrap-around portico.

Soon it was time to get dressed for dinner and the show. Of course by "dressed" I mean merely a shirt with an actual collar and pant legs that reached all the way to my ankles. Resplendent in my grown-up shirt and largely unwrinkled khaki pants, I strolled (if it can be said that Walter Brennan ever "strolled" after riding a bike all day) to the Inn at 202 Dover—a beautifully refurbished 1874 mansion, now a B&B that quietly dominates the corner of Dover and Hanson streets a block east of the Tidewater. There, at the inn's Peacock Restaurant, I enjoyed a splendid meal of free-range chicken, served with sea-salt-sprinkled asparagus and a heap of macaroni and cheese (clearly the retro side dish de rigueur these days) and a nicely matched glass of organic French sauvignon blanc. Okay, what the heck, two glasses—I'm on foot tonight.

Then it was showtime at the Avalon—two mesmerizing hours under the spell of jazz great Monty Alexander, the Jamaican pianist who has shared the stage and studio with everyone from Frank Sinatra to Dizzy Gillespie.

It was the perfect coda for my Easton adventure, made all the more memorable when I ran into Alexander and his drummer the next morning at the Coffee Cat. They were grabbing a quick bite before heading to the airport and, eventually, Chicago. I was grabbing a quick bite before heading to Easton Point Marina, and, eventually, Annapolis. Speaking of which . . . have I mentioned that Easton is in fact accessible by water? That's what I've been trying to tell people since 1710. Turns out I was right, and I like being right.

---

This article first appeared in *Chesapeake Bay Magazine* in March 2010. Author T. F. Sayles is editor of the magazine.

*Oxford:*

# 11

## Watching Oxford

*It's hard to find a more genteel place than the three-century-old town of Oxford, Md. The author finds no end of places to sit and watch the world go slowly by, sometimes with canine company, sometime not.*

*by T. F. Sayles*

I don't know about Leroy, but I'd had a very busy morning of sitting and watching things in and around Oxford, Md., so I needed to rest. I needed to . . . well, sit and watch things for a while. Leroy, a very serene black Labrador, and the official sitter and watcher of things at Mears Yacht Haven, seemed to think that was a good idea. So we sat for a spell, the two of us, there on the front porch of the marina office, which is right alongside the fuel dock and therefore happens to be a good watching place.

First came the crabbers, two in a row, the first in a small standard deadrise, the second in an outboard that looked like it once had been a harbor launch of some kind but was now clearly a crabbing boat, full of stacked bushel baskets and rigged with a trot-lining wheel and a home-made canopy. I love watching watermen park their boats—so calmly aggressive with the throttle, but never an ounce more power than they need. And deadly accurate. *Rumble-rumble, coast, pivot, ROAR*, done. Each of them needed gas and ice, and each of them came and went with a minimum of fuss.

Then came the little convoy from North Carolina—a gorgeous Pearson True North and two lesser but similar blue-hulled cruisers. The

Pearson and one of the other boats tied up at the fuel dock and the third circled nearby in Town Creek. It was the distinctive drawl of the lady from the Pearson that made me suspect they were not local boats.

"You sound like you're from a way southern part of Maryland," I said to her as she made an enormous fuss over Leroy.

"North Carolina," she said, looking up and smiling. "Wilmington. We've been up here on the Chesapeake for a couple of weeks now. And *I miss my puppy!*" She said that latter bit right into Leroy's happy face, scratching his ears furiously. "He usually comes along with us, but he couldn't this time because he just had surgery on his knee."

They'd been in Oxford a few days, she said (still mostly to Leroy, making me more than a little envious of him; she was very attractive), and now they were heading to Annapolis. After that, she told us, they'd be going to . . . what's that town above Annapolis?

Leroy had no idea, so I took a stab at it. "Glen Burnie?" I said, wasting a joke. "Baltimore?"

No, that wasn't it.

"Honey," she asked her husband, still pumping gas. "Where are we going after Annapolis?"

"Chestertown," he said. Ah, Chestertown. I guess that's "above Annapolis" . . . if you're from North Carolina. "You'll love the Chester River," I said. Soon the blue-hull convoy rumbled away, out of the creek around the bend into the Tred Avon River, and Leroy and I again had the marina porch to ourselves. "Next time, Leroy," I said, "try not to be such an attention hog. You're not the only one who likes to have his ears scratched, you know."

This low-key but entertaining sit-and-watch episode was typical of my early-June visit to Oxford. It helped, of course, that I had scheduled the trip, quite accidentally, on what turned out to be the three most gorgeous summer days ever recorded in human history. Perhaps I exaggerate, but only a little. The first day was especially stunning—temperatures in the 70s, not a trace of humidity, and a breathtaking afternoon sky, achingly blue and full of cotton-ball clouds. And if you can't just sit and watch the world go by on a day like that—or the two that followed, for that matter—something is drastically wrong.

Like nearby St. Michaels, Oxford is a town that evolved, at least in this century, from fishing village to recreational boating magnet. But it has considerably less peripheral business than St. Michaels. Oxford has boatyard/marinas of course—lots of them—as well yacht brokers and dealers, and a far greater number of inns, B&Bs and restaurants than a year-round population of some 600 would ordinarily justify. But there's not much else in the way of pure commerce in Oxford proper, which occupies a narrow strip of land between the Tred Avon River and Town Creek, as well as a few mostly residential blocks on the east side of the creek. There's one gift shop, one market/deli, one bank and one bookstore. Beyond that, it's just houses, churches and all the requisite civic/cultural things: town hall, police station, fire station, post office, library, museum, yacht club, community center, town park. Of course the town is quite old—one of the oldest in the state in fact. It was settled sometime in the 1650s, though little is known of its early years. The town was incorporated in 1683, and 11 years later it was made one of the colony's two official ports of entry—the other being Annapolis—by the Maryland General Assembly.

My crossing from Annapolis, the day before my visit with Leroy, was an uneventful one. I had fired up *Venture*, one of the Chesapeake Boating Club's Albin 28s, at around 2 p.m., and by 4 or so I was passing through Knapps Narrows. Less than an hour after that I was rounding the first

*Boats lining home docks make for a tranquil waterfront scene on Town Creek.*
*Preceding pages: The bow of a workboat on Town Creek.*

bend of the Tred Avon River and turning into Town Creek, having called ahead for a slip at Mears—the first marina you come to in the gauntlet of marinas that is Town Creek. With *Venture* all snugged in, I untied old Golgotha, my trusty fat-tire bike, and rode off to explore. It's a perfect town to explore by pedal power, coverable pretty much in its entirety without breaking a sweat. Turning left out of Mears's gravel drive, I headed west on the Strand, one of the town's most picturesque waterfront streets, lined with beautiful old houses that look north across a narrow strip of sandy beach and out across the bending, mile-wide Tred Avon.

As I approached Morris Street, the town's main north-south drag, I could see the Oxford-Bellevue Ferry off to the right, pulling away from its dock with one car, a motorcycle and three bicycles aboard. It would put those vehicles ashore at the tiny village of Bellevue across the river. (From there it's about four miles north-northwest to St. Michaels, by way of Bellevue Road and Route 33.) Beyond the ferry dock here on the Oxford side, I could see a small grove of sailboat masts and the gray gables of the Tred Avon Yacht Club, topped with a handsome octagonal cupola.

At the Robert Morris Inn, easy to spot with its ancient mustard-yellow siding, I turned south at Morris Street—making a note to myself that the inn's long west-facing dining porch would be a fine choice for dinner tonight. But first I wanted to get the lay of the land, so I continued along Morris Street and into the heart of Mayberry. That is indeed where I thought I was for a moment as I pedaled up Morris, making my own breeze, the entire street to myself as far south as I could see, dappled light flattering one charming old house after another. After half a mile or so, where the main drag bends east around the workboat harbor and becomes Oxford Road, I continued south on Morris, past Pope's Tavern and Oxford Inn. (Note to self: Another nice front porch; dinner tomorrow maybe?)

A few hundred yards beyond that I turned west on Pleasant Street—very well named, not only because of the lovely dozen or so houses nestled there among the trees, but also because it dead-ends at a tiny waterside pocket park. With a bench. Yes, a sitting-and-watching place, of which I availed myself for half an hour or so, watching boats go by on the Tred Avon and watching exactly nothing happen at the Pier Street Marina just a few hundred feet to the south. This is another good dinner spot, my sources at Mears had told me, namely the Masthead Restaurant, which enjoys a wide-open sunset-lovers view of the Tred Avon.

Following Morris Street to its southern end, I came to the entrance of the Cooperative Oxford Laboratory, a marine biology research facility that dates back to 1960—when marine scientists were scrambling to understand the parasitic diseases suddenly plaguing the Bay's oyster population. Since the late 1980s it has been, as its name suggests, a cooperative effort of the National Marine Fisheries Service and the Maryland Department of Natural Resources—still very much focused on oyster biology and habitat, but also the Maryland base of the National Marine Mammal and Sea Turtle Stranding Network.

With the sun getting ever closer to the far shore of the Tred Avon, I decided it was time to head north again and see about dinner at the aforementioned Robert Morris Inn. I made my way in indirect fashion, though, first detouring east on the cinder path around the soccer fields and ball courts of Causeway Park. Then, making my way north again on Morris Street, I wandered east again for a desultory and ad hoc tour of boatyards.

Turning on Market Street and then again on Bank Street, I soon found myself ogling a pair of exquisite picnic boats at the dock alongside the Hinckley Company, a marina and boatyard that, as its name suggests, specializes in the sales and service of those gorgeous Maine-built boats.

At the end of Bank Street, I turned right on Tilghman Street and soon found myself pedaling past the famous Cutts & Case Shipyard—known far and wide as a builder and restorer of custom wooden boats. This yard is the legacy of the late Ed Cutts Sr., who developed his own patented double-planking construction system for wooden hulls. Cutts was also an expert among experts when it came to restoring wooden boats, and one of his most famous restoration projects is in plain view to the passerby, courtesy of a gigantic paned picture window that faces Tilghman Street. On display there in a very informal museum is *Foto*, the 33-foot Frederick Lord designed chase boat that was built for and made famous by prolific yachting photographer Morris Rosenfeld—and restored by Cutts in the early 1990s.

Turning left on Mill Street, just past Cutts & Case, took me past the sprawling Oxford Boatyard—yet another full-service repair yard and marina—and back to the Strand. Turning right there would have taken me back to Mears Yacht Haven, the northernmost stop on the Oxford marina tour—on the west side of Town Creek, that is. To complete the tour you'd have to cross over to the west side, where you'd find two of the three Campbell yards in town—Campbell's Town Creek Boatyard and Campbell's Boatyard at Jack's Point. The other is Campbell's Bachelor Point, located, as its name suggests, on Bachelor Point at the south end of town, poking out into the Tred Avon near the river's mouth.

But, not seeing a practical way of crossing Town Creek on my bike, and with my stomach now growling, I decided it was time to head to the Robert Morris Inn for dinner and some well-earned sitting-and-watching time. There I brought the day to a proper close, courtesy of Salter's Tap Room and Tavern—named for the establishment's relatively new (since 2010) celebrity-chef-proprietor, Mark Salter, formerly of the Inn at Perry Cabin in St. Michaels.

Since all of the historic homes in Oxford are private residences, the Robert Morris Inn is your best bet for an up-close-and-personal history experience. Built in 1710, the original part of the building was the home of Robert Morris Sr., a shipping agent and, more famously, the father of Robert Morris Jr.—a signer of the Declaration of Independence and the so-called "financier of the American Revolution." If you have any inclination toward claustrophobia, I suggest you avoid the four so-called cabin bedrooms, which even the inn's own literature describes as "extremely

*The view of Town Creek from Bank Street, alongside the Hinckley Company's boatyard and marina.*

small." Go instead for the larger captain rooms—or the admiral rooms, which are part of the original 1710 structure.

But I had my own slightly claustrophobic sleeping quarters waiting for me at Mears—the Albin's V-berth—so I was here for dinner only. And an excellent one it was—a lovely glass of pinot noir, a delicious plate of local-flounder fish and chips (not with coleslaw but with peas; a sure sign of an Englishman in the kitchen) and . . . all right, twist my arm, another glass of pinot.

———————

The morning of day two found me right back on the porch of Robert Morris Inn, this time savoring a pancake breakfast and a river view dominated by Optis—the Tred Avon junior sailing program in high gear, no doubt. I enjoyed the view, and the pancakes, and the coffee, and a little more coffee. Then it was off for another day of two-wheel exploring.

First on the agenda for today was the Oxford Museum, just three blocks away on Morris Street. Along the way I stopped for quick looks at three of the towns privately owned historic properties—the Grapevine House just up and across from the inn, then the Academy House in the next block and, a few doors farther on the east side of the street, the Barnaby House. This latter, built in 1770 by sea captain Richard Barnaby, is on the National Register of Historic places and is considered by the Maryland Historic Trust to be the town's best example of 18th-century architecture—that is, the least modified over the years. The Grapevine house, dating from 1798, gets its name from the 200-year-old grapevine that still grows in its front yard, brought from the English Channel island of Jersey in 1810.

The 1848 Academy House (aka the Bratt Mansion) was built as an officers' residence for the short-lived Maryland Military Academy— established in 1848 by General Tench Tilghman of Oxford, grandson of Colonel Tench Tilghman, who had been George Washington's aide-de-camp during the Revolutionary War (more on Tilghman later). Opened with the purpose of training young gentlemen "in the southern sense," whatever that meant at the time, the academy only lasted until September of 1855, when its dormitory and classroom building burned down. The school never reopened, and the house was bought in 1862 by Henry and Jane Bell of Ireland, as a wedding present for their daughter Mary Ann, who had come to live in Oxford with her new husband, an English immigrant by the name of Samuel Bratt. Hence the alternate name.

This latter bit I learned not by osmosis from the sidewalk in front of the house, but from the Oxford Museum—where hang individual portraits of those generous parents, the "Bells of Ireland." On duty that day at the museum was the director herself, Ellen Anderson. The modest storefront museum opened in 1964, she told me, and has been amassing Oxford artifacts and oddities ever since. "We're an all-volunteer organization," she said. "Unlike some larger museums, we get no county, state or federal support. So, all things considered, we do pretty well."

Among the artifacts and displays are a French-made fourth-order Fresnel lens from the Benoni Point lighthouse that was destroyed by an ice floe in 1908; a display of wooden boatbuilder's tools, photos of Downes and Albert Curtis, famous African-American sailmakers who ran their business for many years from a Jim Crow era schoolhouse in Oxford that had operated for blacks only until 1937; photos and artifacts from the town's commercial heyday, the late 19th-century, when oysters were plentiful and railroad lines grew like kudzu; and of course displays on the two names that come up in even the briefest history of Oxford— Robert Morris Sr. and Tench Tilghman.

The grave site of the latter, at the sprawling Oxford Cemetery on the opposite side of Town Creek, was well worth the trip, Anderson said. So, not being one to take local knowledge for granted, I headed there next. This time I bore left at Pope's Tavern (addendum to earlier note to self: yes, definitely dinner there tonight; it looks fun) and pedaled east along Oxford Road, past the Oxford Community Center (addendum to addendum to note to self: stop there too, to see what's what; I'd read somewhere that the community center was an old school, but this place looks brand-new), past the Fire Department, past a cornfield or two, to Oxford Cemetery Road—a long, string-straight drive with a distinctly formal feel to it, lined as it is with ancient cedars. The Tilghman monument is quite hard to miss, in fact—just to the right of the drive as you begin the one-way loop around the cemetery, which occupies all of the stubby neck of land between the two eastern branches of Town Creek.

I've never met a cemetery that hasn't made me instantly contemplative, if not downright introspective, so I was not surprised by my impulse to plop down in the grass here and contemplate Colonel Tilghman. He was, I'd read, the oldest of 11 children born to James Tilghman on a nearby plantation called Fausley. He was educated in Philadelphia and went into business with an uncle there, but returned to Maryland at the onset of the Revolution. Though his father and many of his siblings remained loyal to Britain, Tench did not; in 1775 he joined the Maryland Militia, which in 1776 became part of the Continental Army, where Tilghman rose to the rank of lieutenant colonel and soon became aide de camp to General Washington himself, a position he held for the rest of the war. Tilghman is most famous for being the officer who traveled to Philadelphia to inform the Continental Congress of the defeat of Lord Cornwallis in Yorktown, Va., despite being sick with "chills and fever." Most accounts suggest that the physical toll of that episode contributed to his early death, at the age of 41, just five years later. Clearly, General Washington thought the world of him. Washington's own words are inscribed on the 10-foot-tall memorial that stands next to the grave, saying, in part: "While living no man could be more esteemed, and since dead none more lamented than Col. Tilghman. No one had imbibed sentiments of greater friendship for him than I had done. He left as fair a reputation as ever belonged to a human character."

As memorial sentiments go, to say nothing of their source, you could do worse, I thought as I climbed back on my bike and headed back to town. Next on the note-to-self agenda was the Oxford Community

*A view of upper Town Creek from one of the town's many great sit-and-take-it-all-in spots.*

Center, just half a mile away on the other side of Oxford Road. There I was fortunate enough to find Barb Seese, the center's gregarious executive director, who quickly cleared up my confusion about this new old school. A sturdy brick affair with a handsome six-column Greek portico facing the road, it is in fact an 84-year-old building—and a historic one at that, built in 1928 as the town's main public school and designed by renowned Maryland architect Henry Powell Hopkins. Hopkins in fact designed several such secondary schools on the Eastern Shore, Seese told me, but this is the last one left in its original form.

And it looks new, she said, because it *is* new, sort of. That is, it has just undergone a nearly $3 million renovation, begun in 2010. The first dramatic chapter in its story was in the early 1980s when the school came very close to being torn down. But Oxford citizens rallied to save the building and put it to use as the town's community center—a role it has served well for 30 years, not least as home of the town's well regarded theater company, the Tred Avon Players. And, now renovated top to bottom, it will continue to serve the theater group, with a much improved 175-seat auditorium, stage and backstage area. But also it will serve more than ever as the town's central gathering place, with more concerts and performing arts, more children's classes and activities, more continuing education classes. More *everything*, Seese said, adding that it will also be the town's official visitor's center.

Back on my bike and pedaling back down Morris Street, I glanced at my watch. . . . Yikes, four o'clock! Where had the day gone? That was a rhetorical question, of course, because I knew it had gone mostly to pedaling around Oxford aimlessly, happily, stopping as the spirit moved me to sit and watch, and then sit and watch some more. But there was one more sit-and-watch place I wanted to check out before the day got completely away from me—the front porch of Pope's Tavern at the Oxford Inn, where perhaps a crabcake and glass of wine might be conveniently placed in front of me.

So I went back to the boat, changed into my big-boy pants, and then doubled back to the tavern, easy to spot because of the Pope's Mobile parked in front. No, not *the* Popemobile. This is the Pope's (Tavern) Mobile, a beautifully restored London Black Cab—1958 Austin, to be exact—that serves as a courtesy car for the tavern and inn (with its seven guest rooms). It looks like something out of a war movie, as if Ingrid Bergman might emerge from it at any minute.

She did not. But the aforementioned crabcake and glass of wine did appear conveniently in front of me, as I'd hoped—and disappeared just as quickly, along with two delicious slices of fried green tomatoes. And that was just the beginning of what turned out to be a splendid evening on the tavern's porch, where I struck up a conversation with Lisa MacDougal and Dan Zimbelman, the married co-owners of the inn and tavern (she the head chef). We chatted the daylight away, sipped wine, smoked a very nice cigar or two. It's hard to imagine a more civilized end to what had already been a very civilized day.

"What a lovely place this is to just sit and watch the world go by," I said to Dan at one point, meaning Oxford as a whole, not just this particular porch. And he must have understood that, because he said, "Yes, it's that kind of town. It's just that kind of town."

---

This article first appeared in *Chesapeake Bay Magazine* in August 2012. Author T. F. Sayles is editor of the magazine.

*Patuxent River:*

# 12

## A Large Fleet, Stalking Through the Wood

*Up the Patuxent and through the woods, to Madison's house we go. . . . Following the British invasion route of 1814.*

*by T. F. Sayles*

"It was a *derecho*!" I had said to myself, out loud, as I sat in the fan-cooled cabin of *Journey* and read yet another account of the British attack on Washington in August of 1814. It hadn't been just any old summer thunderstorm that put a literal damper on the redcoats' pyromania on that August evening almost exactly 198 years earlier; it had been a derecho, something I'd never heard of until late June of this year, when one such fast-moving straight-line storm front came ripping through Maryland and Virginia at highway speed, packing 80- to 100-mph winds that knocked down trees, tore off roofs and left millions of people without power for days on end. Until now, I'd thought it had been a garden variety violent thunderstorm that had helped douse the fires that long ago August afternoon. But no. Christopher George's description in *Terror on the Chesapeake* makes it pretty clear it was much more than that: "The tempest lifted the British 3-pound cannons and hurled them aside like toys. [It] also blew the drums out of camp like paper cups. Trees were uprooted and ships unmasted for miles around. The roof was torn off the patent office, which [the] superintendent of patents had persuaded the British to spare."

Clearly, not a garden-variety thunderstorm. And for some reason that delighted me—that connection, that direct similarity between this summer and that of 1814. Indeed, it became sort of the underlying theme of this expedition. I'd come to Solomons on *Journey*, one of Chesapeake Boating Club's Albin 28s, with the express purpose of following Great Britain's military thrust up the Patuxent River, and then alongside it, two centuries ago. I wanted to see with my own eyes the river and land that had carried those three British brigades—some 4,000 battle-hardened vets of the Napoleonic wars in Europe—to Washington. And making the trek in late August, just as they had, made it feel all the more authentic, made it that much easier to see, or at least imagine, what might have been seen by those British soldiers and sailors, by the disorganized American defenders, by the frightened populace of fishers and tobacco farmers.

Yes, it's the conceit of a true history nerd, but . . . there it is. I admit it. I own it. Weird as it may be, I was delighted to be feeling the same oppressive heat felt by those dreadfully overdressed British soldiers, breathing the same dense summer air, listening to the same deafening swells of cricket song. Dodging the same sudden and raucous summer storms.

And that carried over to the next day and phase one of my first follow-the-Brits expedition. As I motored up the Patuxent out of Solomons, I found myself faithfully following the river's main channel, watching the chartplotter closely so as to stay in the very deepest part of the river, where the British frigates no doubt stayed—or at least tried to—in order not to run aground. And I wasn't even *aware* I was doing this until I was well upriver from Solomons, somewhere in the vicinity of Broomes Island, site of one of the many British raids that spring and summer, at the height of the War of 1812.

———————

But I'm getting a little bit ahead of myself. And by that I don't mean I'm going to anesthetize you now with eight paragraphs on the arcane causes of the war. No, I mean that I had cruised down from Annapolis the previous afternoon, arriving in Solomons just before sunset and securing a slip at the comely Spring Cove Marina on Back Creek. That night, after an excellent dinner at the nearby Stoney's Kingfisher restaurant, I hunkered down in *Journey*'s cockpit, surrounded by the books that had lived on my nightstand for the previous months and would be my tour guides for the next couple of days. Chief among those were: the aforementioned *Terror on the Chesapeake* by Christopher George, written in 2000, which nicely sums up the invasion over the course of three chapters; Donald Shomette's definitive *Flotilla: The Patuxent Naval Campaign in the War of 1812*, first published in 1981 and updated in 2009; and Ralph Eshelman's 2011 *Travel Guide to the War of 1812 in the Chesapeake*. (Left behind on the nightstand, for the sake of traveling light, were the much larger *War of 1812 in the Chesapeake: A Reference Guide to Historic Sites in Maryland, Virginia and the District of Columbia*, a companion to the Eshelman book, which he coauthored with Scott Sheads and Donald Hickey; and *The Rockets' Red Glare: An Illustrated History of the War of 1812*, another 2011 book by Hickey, with coauthor Connie Clark.)

From that night's review emerged what seemed like a reasonable battle plan for the days to come, however many it might take. As the majority of British ground troops had done that summer from Solomons, which is to say the mouth of the Patuxent, I'd follow the river as far as the town of Benedict on the western shore, about a third of the way from Solomons to Washington. From Benedict, I'd follow the Brit's overland path in a rented car—not the exact route, of course, because even the

*Benedict, Md., viewed from the high ground just west of the town.*
*Preceding pages: The view from beneath the Thomas Johnson Bridge near Solomons, which connects Calvert and St. Mary's counties.*

most painstaking historical accounts don't give you that. And even if they did, I'm pretty sure that the folks at the Enterprise car rental office in Lexington Park would take a dim view of me traversing forests and tobacco fields—as the Redcoats clearly did when the dirt roads of the day failed to serve. And eventually, according to the plan, I'd find myself in Bladensburg—where American forces finally made a stand along the upper Anacostia River, known then as the Eastern Branch of the Potomac.

I slept poorly and fitfully that first night in *Journey*'s V-berth, though I don't know why. It's not like me to sleep poorly, and it wasn't the heat, as robust as that had been on this typical August day. The first thing I'd done after tying up and plugging in was open the portlights and put the two fans on high, so it was quite comfortable and well ventilated by bedtime—and even bordering on cool by morning. But it was not a restful night, for whatever reason, and I was out of sorts as I threw off the lines in the morning and headed out Back Creek for the nautical phase of the expedition. But, now that I had my full nerd on, I decided the sour mood was very much in keeping with the mission—because I'd read more than once that the soldiers of the British invasion force sailing up the Patuxent in 1814 weren't feeling all that chipper themselves. All veterans of the ferocious Peninsula War in southern Europe, in which an uneasy British-Spanish-Portugese alliance had defeated France and forced Napoleon's abdication in early 1814, they had spent almost three months crossing the Atlantic. They had been packed into small, crowded ships—fighting off an outbreak of typhus much of the way, according to Christopher George—and were generally very cranky by the time they reached the mouth of the Patuxent.

Perversely, this shared sense of crankiness was its own cure. Just realizing it made me feel better, and before I'd even passed under the soaring Thomas Johnson Bridge, just upstream and around the bend from Solomons, I found new enthusiasm for the mission. It helped that it was a gorgeous day—a bit too warm and steamy for my tastes, but nothing that a constant 12 knots of self-made breeze couldn't mitigate. That was indeed the only breeze to be found, and by the time I reached Broomes Island, seven miles or so upstream, the water had gone glassy smooth. With billowy, cotton-white clouds grandly parading by to the north and east, it was really quite the picture-perfect day—for the moment, anyway.

As beautiful as those clouds were, I knew down to my mid-Atlantic roots they were the kind that could, and likely would, develop purple bel-

lies by mid-afternoon—and make being out on the water less than pleasant, if not dangerous. So there should be no dillydallying, I decided. I'd
head straight for Benedict, the day's most historically important destination. And, depending on whether or not those purple bellies showed up,
maybe I'd be able to squeeze in a side trip up St. Leonard Creek on the
way back to Solomons in the afternoon.

Royal Navy Rear Admiral George Cockburn, despised plunderer of
the Chesapeake and chief proponent of the assault on Washington, had
chosen Benedict as the ideal place for the invaders to go ashore. "I consider the town . . . to offer us advantages for [landing] beyond any spot in
the United States," he wrote his boss, Vice Admiral Alexander Cochrane,
commander of the North American campaign. So, after "stalking through
a wood," for some 17 miles up the Patuxent, in the words of Captain
Harry Smith, an aide to General Robert Ross, commander of British
ground forces, the fleet hove to at Benedict and put some 4,000 soldiers
and marines ashore.

Lieutenant George Gleig, a Scotsman in the British Army's 85th
Regiment and a prolific diarist—frequently quoted in both *Terror on the
Chesapeake* and Shomette's *Flotilla*—described the town as a "small strag-
gling place, the houses of which stand far apart from each other, and are
surrounded by neat gardens and apparently productive orchards."

Benedict remains a small place, likely even smaller, with no orchards
to speak of and houses now very close together—perhaps 100 of them on
a handful of streets on the narrow peninsula separating shallow (upriver)
Mill Creek from the Patuxent River. It lies just below the west shore
landing of the bridge that carries Route 231 across the river from Calvert
County to St. Mary's County. This low-slung bridge with a swing span
in the middle (opening by scheduled request, 410-535-4634) is the only
bridge across the river between Solomons and Upper Marlboro, about 20
miles upstream from Benedict. Easily clearing the bridge's 16-foot vertical clearance in the low-profile Albin, I explored a bit farther upstream,
interested mostly in getting a closer look at the Chalk Point power plant,
looming at the mouth of Swanson Creek about two miles above Benedict
and visible on that clear day from a good 10 miles downriver.

Though some of the shallow-draft boats in the British invasion fleet
went that far upriver, I wasn't nearly so brave. Seeing that the last marker,
red "32", was just two upstream, I decided this was far enough for
history-tracing purposes. Far better—and more authentic even, I

rationalized—to follow the land route from here. So I swung back south and ducked under the bridge again.

I briefly considered tying up at the docks of the Rivers Edge marina/restaurant on the quiet Benedict waterfront, where it appeared there was a good deal of beer available, judging by the Coors and Budweiser billboards facing the river. A bottle of Bud would have really hit the spot at that point . . . but then I noticed the darkish clouds gathering in the western sky, muttering ominously to one another, no doubt plotting to rain on me. Time to head back, I decided, and I pointed *Journey* downriver and skedaddled. It turned out to be an excellent decision, because a furious storm rolled through an hour and a half later, not more than five minutes after I'd gotten settled in my slip at Spring Cove.

On the upside, the storm left behind a beautiful evening, just warm enough for a half-hour float in the marina pool, a little thrown-together dinner in the cockpit, and—with a history book in my lap—the long-awaited beer. Okay, two beers. You've gotta love delayed gratification.

---

The following morning, with a rental car at my disposal, I crossed the Thomas Johnson Bridge into St. Mary's County and headed north on

*The restored one-room Nottingham Schoolhouse, built in 1911.*

Route 235. The plan was to pick up the British overland route outside Benedict and follow it all the way to Bladensburg, Md., just outside Washington. That is where numerically superior but disorganized American forces finally came together to challenge the invaders— unsuccessfully, as you might guess from the battle's derogatory nickname: the Bladensburg Races.

Following the British invasion route is an exercise in approximation, as I mentioned earlier; even if the exact route had been recorded in its entirety back then (it hadn't, though the history books show that British officers were fond of sketching out important bits of it), modern-day roads go their own way. The best guide for this, I had discovered before the trip, was the Google-based map on the website for the Star-Spangled Banner National Historic Trail (*www.starspangledtrail.net/visit-the-trail*)—a printout of which I'd brought along with me.

Starting in Benedict, I headed west, as the invaders had, along what is now Prince Frederick Road (Route 231). Being fresh off the ship and less than fit for a long march, they covered only about four miles that first day, stopping to camp where modern-day Route 381, Brandywine Road, heads north. There they turned north and paralleled the Patuxent (for the sake of naval support) all the way to Upper Marlboro. Nowadays this means following 381 north for about seven miles and then turning on Croom Road where Brandywine Road bends off to the west. After about 12 miles on Croom Road, when you're roughly even with the top of Jug Bay (the river is never more than three miles east of this route), Croom Station Road takes you north into Upper Marlboro.

From there, faithfully following the red line on my Star-Spangled Trail map, I went west on Old Marlboro Pike, Pennsylvania Avenue (Route 4), and Old Marlboro Pike again, and then northish on Silver Hill Road (458), which becomes Walker Mill Road, which becomes Addison Road, which . . . . well, here is where things went wrong. If you know this area at all, you know that by now I was not in Kansas anymore, not out on the rolling roads of rural Prince George's County, where the old tobacco barns still dot the landscape. No, now I was in dizzying downtown P. G. County. If I'd been on my toes, I'd have simply turned right on Eastern Avenue, then picked up the Anacostia Freeway, then turned west on Annapolis Road (450), which merges with U.S. Route 1 at the bridge over the Anacostia River. . . . Which is *exactly where the British troops crossed*, though not before losing dozens of men to artillery fire on what was then a very narrow wooden bridge, because this is where the American forces, a hodgepodge of regular army troops and militia units, finally confronted them.

But I didn't go that way. I chose to get lost instead. Somehow I ended up on Benning Road, sitting in construction traffic at the intersection of . . . oh, Bladensburg Road! That sounds promising. I turned right there and soon found myself passing Fort Lincoln Cemetery. That sounds familiar, I said to myself, pulling into an IHOP parking lot to get my bearings. And sure enough, it was somewhere right around here that the famous Commodore Joshua Barney and his flotillamen—they of the plucky Chesapeake Flotilla, which had tangled with the British Fleet just two months earlier at the two battles of St. Leonard Creek—had set up their cannons on the road and, seasoned artillerymen that they were, at least momentarily halted the British advance. That was the only meaningful resistance the Brits saw, not counting the initial salvos at the bridge—which they quickly bulled across, leaving behind the usual pile of red-coated bodies.

Most of the literature suggests that Barney's position across the road was back west a bit, at the D.C.-Maryland boundary, where the cemetery is now. But I couldn't help but wonder if it mightn't have been right here, out in front of the IHOP. Or maybe a block or so east, at 38th Street, where the road really begins its slope down toward the river, where the commanding view begins, where the artillerymen would have had the clearest shot.

That's what I'm going with, anyway. I'm going to say, with all the relish a history nerd can conjure, that I followed the invasion route start to finish, from the mouth of the Patuxent to Barney's last stand. Right down from the IHOP.

---

*The following are featured points of interest along the Patuxent River War of 1812 Bicentennial Trail.*

## Barney's Second-to-Last Stand

About five miles above Solomons on the east side of the Patuxent River is the long and winding St. Leonard Creek, cutting nearly all the way across lower Calvert County and the peninsula that separates the Patuxent from the Bay. This is where Commodore Joshua Barney holed up with his plucky Chesapeake Flotilla after first clashing with Royal Navy in the Battle of Cedar Point on June 1, 1814—which might have gone better for Barney and the flotillamen if a sudden squall hadn't interrupted the proceedings. The flotilla acquitted itself fairly well later in the same month in the two-part Battle of St. Leonard Creek. Neither of those clashes could be considered decisive, but the second one, on June 26, left one of the British warships badly damaged and allowed Barney and company to escape farther upriver, where the big ships couldn't go.

## To Attack or Not to Attack

"It is quite impossible for any country to be in a more unfit state of war than this is now," wrote Rear Admiral George Cockburn in July of 1814 to his immediate superior, Vice Admiral Alexander Cochrane, the newly appointed commander in chief of the British forces in North America. Cockburn, whose Royal Navy squadron had been blockading the Bay, menacing its shipping and raiding its towns since the spring of the previous year, was now pushing for an invasion of Washington.

Now with some 4,000 ground troops in the theater, fresh from their defeat of Napoleon, Cockburn insisted that it would require only a little "firm and steady conduct" on the part of the British military to have the American upstarts "completely at our mercy." Cochrane was not so certain, nor was Major General Robert Ross, commander of the British ground forces. Nevertheless, they followed Cockburn's advice and put the troops ashore at Benedict and marched them north, letting the Americans guess whether

*A Civil War era cannon at the Fort Lincoln mausoleum.*

they were merely chasing Commodore Joshua Barney's Chesapeake Flotilla, which had tangled with the Royal Navy in June at St. Leonard Creek, or were in fact ultimately planning to attack Washington. Or perhaps Baltimore. Or Annapolis. It wasn't until his three brigades were camped outside Nottingham, 13 miles upriver from Benedict, that Ross decided at last to head for Washington.

## Mount Calvert

Perched on high ground overlooking the Patuxent River and Jug Bay and part of a rich archaeological site, the two-century-old Mount Calvert House a few miles southeast of Upper Marlboro was an obvious site as headquarters for the Prince George's County Historical Society. And that's exactly what it became in 2009. It remains so, but it has been closed to the public since last August, when it suffered significant damage in the Mineral, Va., earthquake that shook most of the Mid-Atlantic. Both chimneys toppled from the house, and it also sustained some foundation damage.

Built in 1789 by tobacco planter John Brown, the house and its occupants were eyewitnesses to the dramatic events of August 1814. They could see and feel the explosions that destroyed Commodore Joshua Barney's fleet of fighting barges, intentionally "blown to atoms" (to use the British naval commander's words) so that they would not fall into enemy hands. The occupants also saw hundreds of British marines and seamen come ashore at the plantation landing, on their way to join the Washington-bound invasion force. While the mansion is closed until further notice, it is only part of the larger Mount Calvert Historical & Archaeological Park, which boasts some 8,000 years of archaeological artifacts, representing American Indian, "Euro-American" and African-American culture (the plantation was a slave-holding operation until the Civil War).

## Nottingham

There's very little to the place now, and it's difficult to even glimpse the river here (the NO PARKING and NO TURN-AROUND signs at the end of Nottingham Road are less than welcoming), but it was a comparatively bustling settlement in 1814, even though its true heyday as a tobacco trading port (since 1706) had passed. Situated on the west shore of the Patuxent about 13 miles above Benedict, this is where Commodore

Joshua Barney's Chesapeake Flotilla holed up after the battles of St. Leonard Creek—until the British troops closed in and Barney was forced to torch his boats. Much of the town was destroyed by a fire in 1901. On the site now is a restored one-room schoolhouse, built in 1911 at a whopping cost of $744.50. It served as Nottingham's one and only school until just after World War II. The school is open by appointment only. 301-464-5291.

## Benedict

The British invasion force landed at Benedict on the afternoon of August 19, 1814, meeting no resistance there—indeed, finding the town largely deserted. Those few inhabitants who remained were more than a little cranky, according to widely quoted diarist Lieutenant George Glieg of the British Army's 85th regiment (who published a memoir years later, recounting his experience in the little American war). They were "surly beasts," he wrote, "sneering at our troops, refusing to even return a greeting, and spitting in a way that showed their detestation." He was a bit more fond of the geography than of the people: "The banks of the river covered with fields of Indian corn and meadows of the most luxuriant pasture, the neat wooden houses, white and surrounded with orchards and gardens, with backgrounds of boundless forest."

Not sure what to expect in the way of armed resistance, the 4,000-plus troops set up a well-defended camp on the heights above town. "On the brow of the hill, and above the centre line, were placed the cannon, ready loaded, and having lighted fuses beside them," Glieg wrote, "whilst the infantry bivouacked immediately under the ridge . . . in order to prevent their disposition to be seen by the enemy, should they come down to attack." They didn't attack; indeed the invaders met virtually no resistance until reaching Bladensburg three days later.

## Now Versus Then

Standing on Bladensburg Road today, whether you're looking east toward the river, from the vantage point of the American forces, or west, from the British viewpoint, it's very difficult to imagine the much more bucolic scene it was in 1814. Back then, from the heights in either direction you could likely see a sprinkling of houses, some facing the river from the east bank, just north of what was then called the Washington Road, and some facing the road itself, also on the north side. It was past these latter that the British charged before crossing the narrow wooden bridge, some time shortly after noon on August 24. The first charge was cut to pieces by a salvo of American artillery, but the seasoned Brits gutted it out and pushed their way across on a second effort. After that they quickly rolled back the defenders, meeting firm resistance only when they approached Commodore Barney's battery, stationed on the road at what is now 38th Avenue. But with the American forces crumbling elsewhere, Barney could only hold this third line of defense for so long, and he himself fell wounded before ordering his troops to withdraw.

## Fort Lincoln and the Barney Memorial

The monument to Commodore Joshua Barney is difficult to find, in the wrong place and somewhat inaccurate in its wording, but aside from that . . . perhaps you'll still find it worth a visit. To do so, go into the main entrance to Fort Lincoln Cemetery (3401 Bladensburg Road), and follow the road off to the right (west) toward the large building atop the hill. That's the cemetery's mausoleum, and directly behind it is a parking lot and the Barney monument. It reads: THIS IS THE SITE OF THE BATTLE OF BLADENSBURG. IT WAS HERE THAT COMMODORE BARNEY AND HIS MARINES WERE DEFEATED IN THE WAR OF 1812. THE BRITISH MOVED ON TO BURN THE CAPITOL AND WHITE HOUSE. Thing is, this isn't really the

*Mount Calvert House a year after the earthquake, it's damaged chimneys mostly rebuilt.*

"site of the battle," though some small part of it may have happened here. And it certainly isn't where Barney set up his artillery battery. That, all of the accounts seem to agree, was directly on what is now Bladensburg Road, at roughly 38th Street, nearly half a mile north of this spot. On the upside, it's a lovely cemetery, built on the site of a Civil War era fort.

---

This article first appeared in *Chesapeake Bay Magazine* in October 2012. Author T. F. Sayles is editor of the magazine.

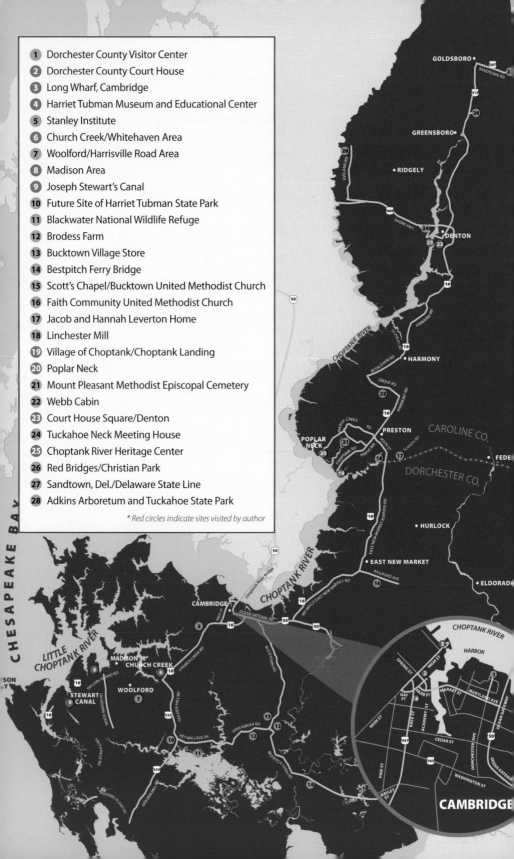

1. Dorchester County Visitor Center
2. Dorchester County Court House
3. Long Wharf, Cambridge
4. Harriet Tubman Museum and Educational Center
5. Stanley Institute
6. Church Creek/Whitehaven Area
7. Woolford/Harrisville Road Area
8. Madison Area
9. Joseph Stewart's Canal
10. Future Site of Harriet Tubman State Park
11. Blackwater National Wildlife Refuge
12. Brodess Farm
13. Bucktown Village Store
14. Bestpitch Ferry Bridge
15. Scott's Chapel/Bucktown United Methodist Church
16. Faith Community United Methodist Church
17. Jacob and Hannah Leverton Home
18. Linchester Mill
19. Village of Choptank/Choptank Landing
20. Poplar Neck
21. Mount Pleasant Methodist Episcopal Cemetery
22. Webb Cabin
23. Court House Square/Denton
24. Tuckahoe Neck Meeting House
25. Choptank River Heritage Center
26. Red Bridges/Christian Park
27. Sandtown, Del./Delaware State Line
28. Adkins Arboretum and Tuckahoe State Park

*Red circles indicate sites visited by author

*Dorchester County:*

# 13 | By Way of Freedom

*A boat trip along the Harriet Tubman Underground Railroad Byway becomes a journey to understanding.*

*by Jody Argo Schroath*

I begin this story where it ended, at anchor in Church Creek off the Little Choptank River. It is late in October, so night has come too soon, but the air is still redolent of summer, soft and close. I'm standing on the front deck of *Zen*, my Endeavor catamaran, staring into the dark, absent-mindedly scanning the inky black shoreline. Around me I hear the ageless night sounds of a lowland marsh: the screech of a night heron, the white noise of frog call, the slap of a hunted fish, the rustle and snap of deer moving through the shoreline underbrush. Pines, oak and maple etch a mountain range of black against an ashen gray-green sky. I am thinking about this project I've just completed, spread out hit or miss over two years. It still envelops me like a bell jar, and I don't want to break its spell. So, standing there in the dark, I begin to tell myself this story. It's a grand story, with a little scaffolding around the outside, which is my part in it. The story I tell is how I discovered the extraordinary life of Harriet Tubman by way of a cruise along the Underground Railroad Byway.

I begin with the knowledge that Harriet Tubman liked to travel on nights like this, as she guided runaway slaves like herself out of Dorchester and Caroline counties into Delaware and Pennsylvania, and finally into Canada, where freedom lay at last. She preferred to move her charges through winter's long nights, despite their bitter cold and dangers. She had the North Star, after all, as well as a strong belief that she was guided by God. Certainly, she drew on her deep knowledge of the Eastern Shore's woods and marshland as she kept her charges just ahead of the slave-catchers and their dogs, fording icy streams and stumbling through dense woods carpeted by sharp and spiny oak and sweet-gum burrs that bedeviled bare feet cracked with cold.

Using an extensive network of safe houses that stretched from Maryland to New York, Tubman led at least 70 slaves to freedom over 13 trips and 11 years. What a remarkable journey it must have been! To free yourself is one thing, but to return time after time for the sake of others, risking capture and re-enslavement each time, is extraordinary. But then Harriet Tubman—Moses to her people, advisor to John Brown, friend to Frederick Douglass, nurse, spy, suffragette and the first woman to lead a military raid—was in all ways extraordinary. How then could I help but be enthralled?

---

My journey began quite without my knowing it two years earlier on a trip up the Choptank River to Denton. There, with follow *CBM* writer Wendy Clarke, I stood in front of the Caroline County Courthouse and read about the site's history as the scene of many a slave auction. It was my first encounter with one of the stops on the Harriet Tubman Underground Railroad Byway. I learned more about Tubman and the Underground Railroad as Wendy and I visited Denton's Rural Life Museum, and yet again, after we had walked across the Choptank bridge to the Choptank River Heritage Center, an old steamboat warehouse from the days when this was a thriving port and shipbuilding center, and where many slaves worked alongside free blacks. Stories of harrowing escapes from slavery and the bravery of Harriet Tubman and others were everywhere, it seemed.

Somewhere during that visit, I acquired a brochure of the Byway driving tour. The Byway, I discovered, covers 125 miles of Dorchester and Caroline counties, from the Little Choptank and Big Blackwater rivers in the south to Sandtown, Del., at the state line to the north. Within those 125 miles, the driving route highlights Tubman's life, first as a slave and then as an agent of freedom for other slaves. Of course, the Byway does not honor Harriet Tubman alone, but also other Maryland Eastern Shore slaves who found their own way or were given instructions by Tubman on how to make their own way through this network—friendly homes and hiding places offered by free blacks and sympathetic whites, especially Quakers, who risked their own lives to help the cause. Studying the map, it didn't take me long to see that water played an important role in the story, which meant that many of the stops were accessible by boat. I had cruised most of these waters before, but this time I would see them with a new eye.

Over the next two years, I visited 10 of the Byway stops, breaking them up in sections and doing them when I could. As I cruised, I also read all I could find about Tubman, but spent most of my time with Kate Clifford Larson's meticulously researched and eminently readable *Bound for the Promised Land—Harriet Tubman, Portrait of an American Hero*, one of the few modern Tubman biographies not written for children. In reading, I also learned about the shape and texture of 19th century life on Maryland's Eastern Shore, and its evolving religious, moral and commercial debate over slavery. And as I read, I began to see the rivers and the landscape of the Eastern Shore as I'd never seen them before—not an especially difficult task, after all, since much of the landscape has changed little in the intervening years.

*Portrait of Harriet Tubman by H. Seymour Squyer, taken about 1885. Preceding pages: A map of the Harriet Tubman Byway.*

In the early years of the 19th century, the Eastern Shore economy had shifted from tobacco to grains, timber and ships. As a result, planters needed fewer enslaved people to do the work, and so not infrequently freed, or "manumitted," them after a certain number of years of service. And so the number of free blacks began to grow. But because most were tied by birth or marriage to those still enslaved, they remained in the area, contributing to the networks of communication that developed over time. The rise of Methodism on the Eastern Shore and its belief in the immorality of slavery also contributed to the manumission of an increasing number of slaves. By 1800 there were 2,365 free blacks in Dorchester County, compared to 4,566 enslaved blacks. (The white population at this time was about 10,000.) This trend in manumission changed after the War of 1812, however, when a severe economic slump threw many Eastern Shore plantation owners on hard times. To relieve their financial distress, an increasing number of slaveholders sold their excess slaves south—a fate that threw terror into the Maryland slave community. Slave auctions were held regularly in towns such as Cambridge, Oxford, St. Michaels and Denton, for buyers supplying the slave-hungry cotton plantations in states such as Georgia, Mississippi and Louisiana. Children could be sold away from their mothers and vice versa. It was also not unusual for slaves who were supposed to have been manumitted at 40 or 50 to be sold (illegally) at 20 as slaves for life. This is what happened to several of Tubman's sisters.

---

Though I have come to it last, Tubman's story begins here, on Church Creek. Harriet Tubman was born Araminta "Minty" Ross sometime around 1822 on the Church Creek plantation of Anthony Thompson, owner of her father, Ben Ross. Church Creek, deeper than it is now, was a busy place in those days, with ships coming and going daily to load grain and timber for market. Ben Ross was a master timberer, a valued slave, and important to his owner's financial success. Tubman's mother, Harriet "Rit," Ross, though temporarily in the same household, was the property of Thompson's second wife and, when he came of age, her son Edward Brodess. Shortly after Minty's birth, Rit and her five children were moved to Brodess's farm on Blackwater Ridge in Bucktown, about 10 miles to the east. It was there that Minty grew up, hired out from childhood to a succession of masters of varying degrees of cruelty to perform a variety of tasks, from household chores to field work.

In about 1835, an event occurred that nearly killed Minty, leaving her damaged for life and forever changing her world view. Hired out to a local farmer, she and the plantation cook were visiting a dry goods store in Bucktown when a local landowner came in to apprehend one of his slaves, who had left without permission. He ordered Minty to hold the boy so he could tie him down, but she refused and the boy sprinted out of the store. The landowner picked up a heavy weight from the counter scale and hurled it after him, but hit Minty instead, fracturing her skull and leaving her unconscious. She was carried back to the farm and left without medical attention. Two days later, still bleeding, she was sent back into the fields. In sorry shape, she was returned to Brodess, who at once tried to sell her, but got no takers because of her condition. Eventually she recovered, but for the rest of her life, she would suddenly fall into a deep sleep for a few minutes every hour or so, even in the middle of a conversation—or an escape. She also was subject to wild visions, with music and voices. These symptoms, biographer Larson writes, are typical of temporal lobe epilepsy. To Minty, though, they were not symptoms of an injury; they were the voice of God, who, she firmly believed, was now guiding her.

———————

Church Creek was the third stop on the Little Choptank leg of my Byway cruise. My first had been two days earlier on Parsons Creek, where I had come to look for the Stewart Canal. Parsons and Slaughter creeks share entrance markers. Winding around green "1", "3" and "5" at the mouth of the Little Choptank, I had turned south off the main channel toward Slaughter Creek markers "2" and "3". I then slipped between markers "4" and "5" and struck off southeast toward Parsons Creek, hoping for the best. Though Parsons was once deep enough for commercial shipping, its upper reaches have long since silted in. Less than half a mile above the "5" the shallow-water warning buzzer sounded and I quickly brought *Zen* to a halt. Down went the anchor, and then the dinghy. Another half a mile up the creek, this time by dinghy, and having scraped bottom only once, I reached the point at which the canal joins the creek after passing under State Route 16. After a few minutes of reviewing all the reasons I shouldn't do it, I spurred the dinghy on up the canal and under the highway.

In the years that followed Minty's injury, she had grown strong, preferring the backbreaking work of timbering, where she was relatively unsupervised, to the lighter but closely watched work of an inside slave. Often she was part of the free black and slave communities—including that of her father—who worked right here, along the Stewart Canal. The seven-mile-long ditch was dug (by slaves of course) over a period of 20 years, to connect the timber-rich land around the Blackwater River with Parsons and Church creeks, which had shipping ports. While working here, Minty met and married free black John Tubman and took the first name Harriet, likely in honor of her mother. At the same time, having gained in skill and experience, she was able to hire out to landowners of her own choosing, by paying Brodess an annual fee for the loss of her service. In this way, she managed to save enough money to buy a pair of oxen, which she used in turn to increase her earnings by plowing fields and hauling timber.

My trip up the canal lasted about two miles, an arrow-straight course through marshland that stretched as far as I could see. Using the trolling motor, I plunged down this narrow avenue, lined by spiky tall reeds that loomed oppressively on either side. I was thankful for the breeze that kept the late-season bitey flies temporarily at bay. Which reminded me that it would be wise to be well away from here and anchored in a good onshore breeze before nightfall. That and the notion of unfavorable tides

Jill Jasuta of Cambridge, Md., at Stewart's Canal. [Photograph by Jim Duffy]

clinched it: time to head back to the boat.

---

Once back aboard, anchor up, I didn't go far. My next Byway stop was Madison, known in Harriet Tubman's time by the more colorful name, Tobacco Stick. I was anxious to do more reading before I wandered through this tiny town at the head of Madison Bay, and I wanted to find that good evening breeze I had been conjuring up on the canal. So I retraced my steps out of Parsons Creek, kissing the bottom this time as I bridged the gap between Parsons Creek and the channel into Slaughter Creek, and returned to the Little Choptank's main channel. Around Susquehanna Neck I went, then past Woolford Neck, before arriving at the broad entrance to Madison Bay with its narrow entrance channel. Not far beyond "2", which marks that whisper thin entrance channel, I found enough deep water out of the channel but still open to the west, where I anticipated a quiet night and a pleasant breeze.

It pretty nearly worked, too. In the morning I awoke with only half a dozen bites—a number I consider tolerable—and happily pulled up anchor to make for shore. At the bottom of the bay, I picked up daymark "4", which marks the beginning of the narrow channel into Madison, and headed for Madison Bay Marina, Restaurant & Campground. The channel is marked at two feet on the NOAA charts, but I've always found it at least a couple of feet deeper, but I'd advise you to keep to high tide, if possible. Now I nudged *Zen* up against the face dock and tied off.

Like Parsons Creek, Madison Bay was once deep enough to support brisk maritime trade, with ships calling regularly to take on grain, fish and timber. As part of this world, Tubman learned much from the many free black mariners who worked aboard the ships—or had ships of their own. From them, she learned about the network of safe houses that followed the water routes north into Delaware and Pennsylvania. She also learned about navigating by the stars, and how to avoid some of the dangers likely to be met by runaways heading north. These black mariners and watermen also were key links in a complex communications network created to circumvent the barriers slavery often put between family members, passing messages and news between separated kin.

There is little left of Tobacco Stick in modern-day Madison—a few homes spread out along the waterfront, a few workboats lying in their slips. There's an old fish- or oyster-house with a loading dock and a couple dozen slips, a picturesque cemetery, fire station, convenience store and the Madison Bay Marina, Restaurant & Campground. Sadly the restaurant, my favorite Madison stop, was closed at the moment, so I dawdled around the cemetery before walking back out the dock to *Zen*. I returned to my previous night's anchorage . . . and to my book.

---

From 1847, the focus of Tubman's life shifted several miles to the north. Dr. Anthony C. Thompson, who had by then inherited his father's slaves and property, bought large tracts of land along the Choptank River at Poplar Neck, 10 miles north of Cambridge. Here he moved most of his male slaves to timber and farm. His female slaves remained to a large degree with Thompson's wife at their townhome in Cambridge. Harriet's father Ben, who had been freed in 1840 and stayed in the Stewart Canal area, now moved north to Poplar Neck to help Thompson, who also gave his former slave 10 acres and a small house.

By contrast, fortunes for the Brodess family, owners of Rit and her children, had gone from bad to worse. Ever in dire financial difficulty, Edward Brodess died in 1849, leaving his wife Eliza deeply in debt. She at once began trying to sell off some of her slaves, including members of Harriet's family. On learning that they were about to be sold, Harriet and two of her brothers, Ben and Henry, ran away on September 17. But after two weeks, fearing capture and not wanting to leave their own young families, the brothers decided to return, bringing an unwilling Harriet back with them.

A month later, Harriet ran away again, on her own this time, telling no one of her plans. Leaving probably from Thompson's Cambridge home, she traveled at night, likely passing through the sympathetic Quaker community of Marshy Creek near Poplar Neck before moving farther north. She was directed each night to a new safe home, until she finally reached Pennsylvania and freedom. Later she described her feelings at that exhilarating moment to her early biographer Sarah Bradford: "When I found I had crossed the line, I looked at my hands to see if I was the same person. There was such a glory over everything; the sun came like gold through the trees, and over the fields, and I felt like I was in Heaven."

---

Cambridge is the site of three stops along the Underground Railroad Byway—four if you count the Dorchester Visitor Center. I arrived there in early October, traveling from Annapolis on *Zen* with Kathy Slack, a friend from way back in college. Following the markers off the Choptank River into Cambridge's broad harbor, we came at once to the first of the three stops, Long Wharf. Here, during the 18th century, ships brought newly enslaved people from Africa to be auctioned in front of the Dorchester County Courthouse. And here, in the 19th century, after the import of slaves was outlawed in 1807, ships departed with local slaves sold to buyers for plantations of the South.

Instead of entering the harbor, Kathy and I peeled off toward Cambridge Municipal Marina. Tied up, we followed the seawall to the harbor.

After a conscientious study of the historical markers along Long Wharf, we headed into town. Cambridge, we decided, was nearly the perfect place to be when you are trying to get a feel for the past. Walking up any of the streets from the waterfront introduces you to an earlier century. Elegant sycamores shade streets that are lined with fine old homes—though not all of them antebellum, of course. We passed first through Long Wharf Park, which parallels the marina, and then took Mill Street to Church Street, where we turned left and followed it until we reached the elegant Romanesque building of the Dorchester County Courthouse, our second Byway stop. This courthouse was built in 1854 after an arsonist set the original on fire in 1852, destroying 200 years of court and land records.

It was here that Tubman's niece Kessiah Bowley and her two small children were to be put up for auction in 1850 by Eliza Brodess. Tubman, now living in Philadelphia, learned about the auction and at once set about making plans for Kessiah's escape. For Tubman, the decision to help was unarguable: If she was free, then her family must be free as well. To earn money for the rescue, she took work in Philadelphia households and hotel kitchens. With the money saved, Tubman went down to Baltimore to wait. When the auction for Kessiah and her children came, the bidding was brisk and a sale quickly concluded. Kessiah and her children were then taken from the front steps to the side of the courthouse while the auctioneer went to lunch. When he returned, the buyer—who was in fact Kessiah's free husband, John Bowley—could not be found. The auctioneer promptly reopened the auction, but by this time Kessiah and her children were nowhere to be found. They were hiding in a house, only minutes away. That night John Bowley sneaked his family into a log canoe and set sail for Baltimore, where they were met by

Tubman, who took them north to Philadelphia and freedom.

A few months later, Harriet orchestrated the escape of her brother Moses, again awaiting him in Baltimore. In 1851, she returned for the first time to the Eastern Shore, this time to bring her own husband away. She had saved the money for the trip and bought him a new suit, but when she arrived, she learned that he had already remarried and didn't want to leave. Likely brokenhearted, she nevertheless stayed focused on the job at hand; she put together a group of slaves who did want to leave and led them north.

After the passage of the Fugitive Slave Act in 1850, Philadelphia was no longer a safe haven for runaway slaves, since they could legally be recaptured and dragged back. So late in 1851, Kessiah and John Bowley and many others moved again, this time to Canada, to start over once more.

Kathy and I spent some time walking around the grounds of the Dorchester Courthouse and walked the few blocks to the Harriet Tubman Museum and Culture Center, our third Cambridge stop. There we spent the remainder of the afternoon, watching a video about Tubman, studying the exhibits and visiting with volunteer and longtime Tubman activist Bill Jarmon. We also found out more about the new Harriet Tubman State Park in the Blackwater National Wildlife Refuge, to be dedicated later this year. This month, it should be noted, marks the 100th anniversary of Tubman's death.

---

The tiny town of Choptank, 10 miles upriver from Cambridge, was next on my list of must-see stops on the Byway. I went by car rather than boat, however, because the small municipal marina is too shallow for *Zen*. I might have been able to anchor out in the river, but the current is swift and the river deep as it swings around the bend at Bow Knee Point (I'm not making that up), and so the weather would have had to be just right. I didn't want to take the chance of missing this stop, because it was from Poplar Neck, just upriver, that Tubman engineered two important escapes—those of three of her brothers and, finally, her parents. The tiny settlement of Choptank was known then as Leonard's Wharf and it served as a shipping port for the nearby town of Preston. Anthony C. Thompson's Poplar Neck home still sits off Poplar Neck Road, which leads north out of Choptank. Harriet's father Ben's small cabin was somewhere nearby.

I arrived on a blustery gray day in early fall, with scudding clouds and glimpses of sun across the river. I walked the empty docks, scattering legions of gulls as I went.

After her first successes, Tubman continued to risk her life and freedom by returning to the Eastern Shore to free others. Many of these trips were made to try to free her sister Rachel, whose sale had been advertised several times. But Rachel and her children were often kept miles apart, so Tubman's efforts were unsuccessful. But each time Tubman would fall back on plan B and lead others north to Canada instead. Then she would start over, earning or raising the money for another rescue trip. As time went on, her fame and stature in the national abolitionist movement grew, and in the community of freed slaves, she was soon called Moses.

During this time, Harriet's mother Rit was able to spend time with her husband in their Poplar Neck home, probably because she had been hired out to the Thompsons. Meanwhile, Harriet's brothers Ben, Henry Ross and Robert, under threat of sale by Eliza Brodess, tried several times to engineer their own escape, but they were either caught immediately or returned home after weeks in hiding. Harriet tried to get them away early in 1854, but failed, instead bringing out Winnibar Johnson of Tobacco Stick. When she heard that her brothers were to be auctioned over the

*Glistening workboats line the shore in Madison, Md.*

Christmas holidays, however, she made plans to return for another attempt.

The brothers were planning to meet for Christmas dinner at their parents' cabin at Poplar Neck, so Harriet arranged for them to gather instead in a corncrib near the house—so that her mother would not know they planned to flee and raise any alarm with her distress. Harriet's father, Ben, knew of the plan, however, and helped by bringing his sons food. To protect himself and them, the story goes, he refused to look at them, so he could truthfully claim later that he hadn't seen them. In the pouring rain, they waited for darkness to leave. Through the loose-fitting planks of the corncrib walls, Harriet, who had not seen her mother in five years, could see her now, watching anxiously for her sons to arrive for dinner. Later, with her mother inside rocking nervously, fretting over what had become of her children, Harriet and her brothers, along with some of their family members and several of their friends began their journey north. The elder Ben, blindfolded, walked several miles with them before saying good-bye. Reluctantly, they left him, standing alone in the middle of a field, his blindfold still in place until they were well out of sight. Tubman led her group to Wilmington, Del., and then Philadelphia, where they chose new names before continuing to New York and Canada. The following year, Ben the elder finally was able to purchase his wife's freedom, though the two, now in their seventies, continued to live and work at Poplar Neck. Their property became part of the Underground Railroad.

Two years later, after several more trips to bring out more family members and others—though still not able to bring away Rachel and her children—Harriet heard that her father might soon be arrested for helping runaway slaves. Now, she felt, she had to get her parents away, despite their age and infirmities. Arriving at Poplar Neck, Tubman found that her mother wouldn't leave without her few precious possessions, nor Ben without his prized broad axe. So Tubman fitted an old horse with a kind of straw collar attached to a pair of old carriage wheels, with a sitting board fit over the axle, and in this way the three made their way north to Canada. There her parents stayed, while Tubman made several more trips and helped dozens of additional slaves escape.

Finally, facing increasing vigilance by slave owners and now with the responsibility of supporting aging parents, Tubman remained in Canada, working to raise funds for arriving escapees, until the start of the Civil War.

---

I end this story where it began, on Church Creek. On the last morning of my Byway trip—this morning—I had packed up Larson's biography and taken the dinghy a short way up Church Creek to the dock off Old Trinity Church—which has been there since 1692 and which saw all of this misery and joy unfold as it came. I found a tree that looked nearly as old as the church's graveyard and settled down to finish reading *Bound for the Promised Land.*

In many ways, Tubman's story is only halfway told when it ends with her final trip to the Eastern Shore. It leaves out her friendship with abolitionist John Brown, who called her "General Tubman," and her extraordinary work during the Civil War in South Carolina as a nurse, spy and leader of a successful military raid. The end of the war saw Tubman tending the sick and wounded at Fort Monroe in Hampton, Va., and traveling to Washington to press Secretary of War William Seward for improved medical care. It leaves out her involvement in the women's suffrage movement and her establishment of a home for aged and indigent freed slaves. And even that doesn't tell it all.

I finished the book and walked slowly through the graves and back to the dinghy. In the evening, I stood on the deck, watching the dark and telling myself this story. Now that I'm finished, I think I'll pull out the charts and see if it can be done . . . coastal Carolina, Fort Monroe, Washington, D.C. Yes, I think I can do it.

This article first appeared in *Chesapeake Bay Magazine* in March 2013. Jody Argo Schroath is senior editor of the magazine and editor of its annual *Guide to Cruising Chesapeake Bay.*

*St. Mary's City:*

# 14

## Cruising in the Company of Saints
*A summer day on the St. Marys River, where the only impediments to heaven are heat and hunger.*

*by Jody Argo Schroath*

Everything was serene in the land of the saints. As serene as hell. First, it was about as hot as the Inferno's eighth ring (in case you lost count, that's the one where the great sailor Ulysses is eternally slow-roasted for his part in the Trojan War). Second, it was humid enough to bathe in. Third, there was no wind. And fourth, I was beginning to quote poetry. Saints, preserve us!

It had begun well enough. My husband Rick and I, along with our friend Hal, had decided to celebrate a kind of midsummer All Saints Day by cruising the St. Marys River and visiting its related nominal holinesses—St. Mary's College, Historic St. Mary's City, St. George Creek, St. George Island and St. Inigoes Creek—names further sanctified by being crucial to Maryland's founding story. Maryland's first settlers landed on St. Clements Island, but learned that the Yaocomaco Indians were holding a kind of going-out-of-business sale along the St. Marys River (not its name then, of course) because the tribe wanted to consolidate its numbers farther upriver as protection from attack by another more fearsome Native American organization. In addition to the land, the Indians also threw in their old houses and all their cultivated fields, so the newcomers pulled out their chests of pretty beads and closed the deal. Then they named everything in sight for various saints and settled down to make a new colony.

On the morning before the official cruise was to begin, Rick and I sailed across the Potomac from the Yeocomico (same Indians, different side of the river) and then idled away the long, still afternoon with iced drinks and good books under the ancient oaks at St. Mary's Yachting Center on Carthagena Creek. (Carthagena was named by William Hebb II for a spectacularly unsuccessful 1741 battle fought for the Caribbean port of Cartagena during the War of Jenkin's Ear by the British—with the aid of colonists such as Hebb and Lawrence Washington—against the Spanish. Nothing came of the war, and Jenkin's ear was eventually pickled.)

Hal arrived on his powerboat early the following morning, which dawned clear and promising, but dead calm, prompting us to opt for a Saints Day cruise by power rather than sail. The three of us set off in Hal's boat with the rising sun and a second cup of coffee. We began our cruise with a perfectly agreeable tour of St. Inigoes Creek—the first creek to the right as you come up the St. Marys. (Inigo is Spanish for Ignatius, so the creek was actually named for Ignatius Loyola, founder of the Jesuit order. A Jesuit priest arrived with the first settlers in 1634, and the Jesuit order in the years that followed held thousands of acres in this area—as well as the entirety of St. George Island, which was more impressive then than it is now since it used to be considerably larger.)

Serene? Very. Up one branch and then another we went, enjoying the quiet, long-settled, woodsy character of houses that lined St. Inigoes— like so many Maine lake cottages—while remarking on the dozen or so new docks, long steep stairs and walkways of the creek's new construction. We also noted several fine potential anchorages—particularly a wooded spot at the top end of Lucas Cove that already had a temporary resident, a lone cruiser who resolutely refused to look up from his book as we motored slowly by, waving futilely. All this while, however, we kept an eager eye on a military helicopter that was doing dramatic touch-and-goes at Webster Field, part of the Naval Air Warfare facility at Priests Point. No welcome mat on their doorstep for cruisers, of course, but the inadvertent air show was free for the viewing. Next door to the Navy, on Molls Cove, the St. Inigoes Coast Guard station was as peaceful as its Maine cottage neighbors this weekend morning. The facility serves the Potomac and its tributaries from Point No Point and Smith Point near the river's mouth all the way up to the U.S. Route 301 bridge.

Two homes along St. Inigoes Creek are worth particular note. Rose Croft graces the point of the same name at the northern entrance of the creek and was the seat of the Maryland colony's first collector of revenue. (Ships coming up the Potomac were supposed to stop here to be taxed—cannons were pointed toward the river to encourage cooperation. But those ships bound for Virginia ports simply hugged the opposite shore and so kept well out of range of both cannon fire and tax collection.) Farther up St. Inigoes, on the opposite shore, sits Cross Manor, probably the oldest home in Maryland, its original parts dating to the late 17th century. It is now owned by newsman Ted Koppel and his wife.

Things were still as serene as Buddha as we left St. Inigoes Creek to work our way up to the navigable limits of the St. Marys River. Passing Chancellor Point, we remained theologically neutral and took Pagan and Church points right down the middle. (The two points, which jut out from either side of the river, offered the new settlement of St. Mary's excellent protection from potential enemies, such as Spanish, Dutch and Virginia Protestants.) Just beyond these points, we emerged into Horseshoe Bend, where the river changes direction from north to northwest.

Once we had gotten about as far upriver as we could, about two

*Ghost frames in the historic St. Mary's settlement.*
*Preceding pages: Sailing dinghies lined up along the St. Mary's College docks.*

nautical miles, we gingerly circled Tippity Wichity Island—a notoriously shallow area with the added menace of an overhanging power line crossing from the northeast shore. (This unassuming geographic feature was once an intriguing blot on the local landscape known as Happie Land, established after the Civil War by a Confederate smuggler named Howgate, who changed the name of the island from Lynch to Tippling-house and Witchery-house Island—hence Tippity Wichity. Or at least that's the story.)

Serenity onboard was wearing thin as we began our trek back down-river, past points Long and Short, and entered Horseshoe Bend once more. The light morning breeze had petered out at 10:15, as punctual as a Swiss train, and we had entered that brief breathless purgatory before the temperature soars and the day goes well and truly downhill.

Hal was steering us well clear of the shoal waters that trail off Horse-shoe Point, when the sun topped out for the day. The humidity and the temperature kept up their neck-and-neck race for 100 as we idled across Horseshoe Bend. It was at this point that serenity flew out the window.

Sweating and sulky, I found myself questioning the very nature of cruising—you know, the whole "Why are we here?" and "What's the point?" revisionist talk. As Rick and Hal looked on helplessly, I began reciting Edna St. Vincent Millay's *The Unexplorer*, which you'll be happy to know is very short because I'm going to quote it:

> *There was a road ran past our door*
> *Too lovely to explore.*
> *I asked my mother once—she said*
> *That if you followed where it led*
> *It brought you to the milkman's door*
> *(That's why I haven't traveled more.)*

Maybe the mother was right, I whined. Maybe all we're doing is motoring by hundreds of Elsie and Elmer homes, I said, referring to the famous Borden spokescows. Sure, it's all nice and pretty, but so is Dubuque. And so forth. . . .

Well, as it turned out, the fault lay not in bovine TV stars, but in my stomach. I didn't suddenly hate cruising, I was just very hungry. And fortunately there are few things that a good $6.50 all-you-can-eat college buffet can't cure.

On reaching Horseshoe Bend, Hal headed directly for St. Mary's

College docks, carefully dodging an outgoing fleet of Special Olympians on the way in, and we went ashore. Providentially, a sophomore political science major from the D.C. area promptly materialized and, taking us figuratively in hand, led us by the shortest possible route to the college commissary. Half an hour and four slices of fresh vegetarian pizza later, life was great and Elsie and Elmer had re-established themselves as fascinating reasons to explore the world.

Call it a minor miracle if you like, but then St. Mary's College of Maryland has always come down on the side of the angels as far as cruisers were concerned. Not only does the college invite cruisers to tie up at the college docks during the day (no overnights, though), it also welcomes them to use the athletic facilities at $5 a day and make use of its showers, as well as the cafeteria, coffee shop and bookstore. If the college docks are full, no problem, there is enough room in Horseshoe Bend for the entire Pacific Fleet to drop anchor (okay, a few of the aircraft carriers might have to wait outside) and dinghy ashore. There is plenty of room at the sandy beach nearby for dinghies.

"The school has always looked to the water," college President Jane Margaret O'Brien told me when we talked the following week. "All the old buildings face the river because that's the way students saw the school—from the water—until 1934, when the steamship stopped running." It's a question of hospitality in a very rural area, O'Brien continued. The college continues to maintain a close relationship with the water; its sailing team, with 13 national championships, is ranked number one in the country.

---

For a place that's pretty much the last stop before the end of the road, St. Mary's was humming on this summer day. The Special Olympians we had encountered on the way in were part of a weekend of racing on a variety of watercraft for the state Special Olympics championships. Next door to the college, Historic St. Mary's City was hosting its annual Archaeology Weekend, which lets visitors sift for themselves among the potsherds and get a once-a-year look at the site's artifact filing system— housed in the climate-controlled basement of a former house.

All of this brings up another benefit of the college's enlightened attitude toward cruisers. Because docking is available, cruisers can easily visit Maryland's fascinating first capital—a feat rarely possible at the nation's other historic sites, which have turned their back on their maritime origins. All of which made our visit to Archaeology Weekend a walk in the park . . . then a short stroll through Trinity Church cemetery, a trek past the Woodland Indian Hamlet, and a hike up the hill to the Visitor Center. At the end of it all—including a short drive by van just a spit down the road—stood curator Silas Hurry, quiet-spoken, earnest and full of the milk of good public relations kindness. He had an eager audience. A few took notes. Here are Cliff's: All of the samples from each dig are clearly marked, sifted, categorized, stabilized, identified, computerized and stored. Now pay attention, because this will be on your final: Archaeologists are now leaving as much of the land as possible undisturbed for future archaeologists because they will presumably know more and have better equipment than today's batch, just as we have it all over the former fellows, who did regrettable things like toss out all the soil that had been turned over regularly in cultivation—soil that, it turns out, actually contains the bulk of what is now considered the good stuff. And like oyster shells, which, it turns out, are important indicators of the health of the Bay because you can measure their rings (kind of like trees, apparently) and thickness and so forth. Because oyster shell fragments

*Grave markers at Trinity Church cemetery.*

were about as common as cucumbers in a pickle factory, nobody ever thought it worth the trouble to collect them—except Historic St. Mary's City archaeologists, who did hang on to them and who can be excused for feeling just a little smug about the whole thing. So, never throw out anything, no matter how dumb it seems—but only if you're an archaeologist. End of lesson.

Following our entertaining encounter with dirt and historic debris we retraced our steps, more slowly this time, to visit Historic St. Mary's City. The town, founded in 1634, was a briefly thriving community that was relegated to the trash heap of history a mere 90 years later when the Protestants gained sufficient power and influence to insist that the center of power for the colony be moved north to the more malleable city of Annapolis. The jilted capital soon faded into memory and its plowed fields, homes, businesses and government buildings forgotten. (The college, in fact, was established as a kind of consolation prize for the lost capital, starting life in 1840 as a girls seminary and ending up as the state's public honors college. So over the years, the school and the lost city have maintained a uniquely special relationship, with their property, interests and activities widely overlapping.)

St. Mary's City was never a city in the sense of a downtown, suburbs and business district. Even at its peak it was only a few dozen homes, a couple of taverns and a state house. The state house was rebuilt in 1934, but most of the other original buildings have been reconstructed only in an outline form called "ghost frames," which gives the impression of a bankrupt 17th century housing development.

An important feature of St. Mary's rebuilt past is the *Dove*—the maritime cargo van that accompanied the first settler's Greyhound bus, the *Ark*. When not showing off elsewhere, the *Dove* is generally parked at a pier not far from the original landing place and at the bottom of a steep descent from the bluff where the "city" stood. On the weekend following our visit, the *Dove* would be out on the river, serving as the finish line for the 34th annual Governor's Cup, a perennially popular overnight sailing race from Annapolis to St. Mary's (from one capital to another)—a distance of about seventy miles, if you don't count all the extra miles required on those many occasions when a beat to windward is the only way down the Bay. The race is sponsored by St. Mary's College and culminates in what has been called one of sailing's top 10 parties.

It was time for us to move on—we still had one more saint waiting in the wings—so we took a final scenic look down at the river from the Margaret Brent Gazebo. (Brent was named executor of the will of Colonial governor Leonard Calvert, Lord Baltimore's son. In 1648 she went before the General Assembly to ask for two votes, one as executor and one as landowner in her own right, and received nothing in return but huffy male disdain.) Back at the college waterfront, we danced inelegantly across the coal-hot sand and returned to Hal's boat. Special Olympics sailors by this time were off the water and had gathered with friends and families in the shade for the awards announcements. The sound of cheers and applause wobbled through the humidity to follow us down the dock.

Once out in Horseshoe Bend, Hal opened the throttle a little more than careful tourism might recommend, but we reveled in the resulting breeze and turned south for St. George Creek. We made two concessions to speed along the way. The first was to admire Porto Bello, the historic estate built in the 1740s by William Hebb II and extensively restored over the past several years by former *Washington Post* editor Ben Bradlee and his wife, writer Sally Quinn. The estate sits on a bluff above the river's western shore. (Porto Bello, like Carthagena, was named by Hebb for yet another battle in the War of Jenkin's Ear—this one a British victory.) Our second tangent was to trace Carthagena Creek past Josh Point, where the creek seems to end before it begins, around the dogleg to the right that materializes at the flashing red "4" to Dennis Point, past private docks and comfortable cottages, and finally turning back as the creek shallowed out beyond Walnut Point.

Now it was simply a matter of keeping the three green markers (two locals and flashing green "1") to our right and then resisting the urge to make our turn into St. George Creek before we had reached red "A". You can get away with the shortcut if you know what you're doing, but we did not. So we played it by the numbers and split the difference between "A" and flashing green "1".

St. George Creek feels nice and roomy for much of its four and a half nautical miles, as it separates first St. George Island and then Piney Point from the Maryland mainland. It's a busy working waterway, too. As we slowed down just before reaching green "1" to try to catch a glimpse of Camp Merryelande at the southern tip of St. George Island, workboats and fishing boats bustled around us and kept us bobbing and binocular bruised. Merryelande, now a private facility with brightly colored rental cabins with varying degrees of civilization and tents, a sandy beach and a fishing dock, was for many years a girls' summer camp operated by Roman Catholic nuns. (The Jesuits were St. George Island's first European inhabitants. They kept herds of Elsies and Elmers on the island because of its abundance of tasty grasses.)

The dominant feature on St. George Creek is the Paul Hall Center for Maritime Training and Education and Harry Lundeberg School of Seamanship. This training complex can be seen from either side of St. George Island and, on a clear day, from well out on the Potomac. The school, which trains merchant seamen for employment on U.S. flagged commercial vessels, is generally closed to visitors, but a slow pass by the docks is a good alternative.

As St. George Creek narrowed and we slowed to keep down our wake, the temperature onboard began to rise as quickly as the cumulonimbus clouds to the west. Pretty soon now, it would behoove us to get off the river. Late afternoon in midsummer is no time to be lollygagging along sightseeing. So we made one quick side trip into Tarkill Cove on the mainland side of the creek then headed for home—St. Mary's Yachting Center, in this case. We had just enough time to put up the awning over the cockpit of the sailboat and pull three greenies out of the cooler before the first storm barreled through. As we put our feet up and watched the rain fall, we agreed with generations of boaters before us that discussing a day spent on the Bay over a cold beer in the sudden coolness of a late afternoon shower is pretty close to heaven. Yep, everything was serene here in the land of the saints.

This article first appeared in *Chesapeake Bay Magazine* in October 2007. Jody Argo Schroath is senior editor of the magazine and editor of its annual *Guide to Cruising Chesapeake Bay*.

*Crisfield:*

# 15

## Nowhere to Go but Upscale

*With the seafood industry in decline, Crisfield, Md., may soon profit from a different kind of catch.*

*by Jody Argo Schroath*

It was a perfect spring day—presidential blue sky, congenial 10-knot breeze straight out of the heart of Dixie, temperature comfortably in the porch-rocker 70s. In fact, it had all of the ingredients you would throw into your January daydreams to produce the ideal first cruise of the year. Of course, it had taken its sweet time getting that way. Dense fog had kept us— my cruising buddy Hal, ship's dog Skippy and me—cooling our heels since early morning, first at the mouth of the Yeocomico and then at the mouth of the Potomac, waiting for visibility to improve before poking our nose out into the Bay. But our patience had been rewarded at last, and here we were in the middle of the Chesapeake—with Point Lookout aft and Smith Island fore—on our way to Crisfield for the very first time.

Now, among Chesapeake Bay boaters, having never been to Crisfield is like a French person never having been to Paris. No, that's not right. Annapolis has got to be Paris for a Chesapeake boater, so that would make Crisfield more like Marseille. Crisfield, like Marseille, was built on maritime trade and it is on the southern end—of Maryland, in this case, instead of France. Okay, and it's not on the Mediterranean, either. Look, forget I brought it up.

Crisfield, which is known everywhere on the Bay as "the town that used to be known as the Seafood Capital of the World," was built on the triumvirate of oysters, terrapins and crabs. Only crabs, that Julius Caesar of seafood, have survived in any useful numbers. But Crisfield, too, has survived, though it has long since been demoted from seafood capital to quaint former seafood capital. But that in no way has diminished its appeal to boaters on the Bay. In fact, quaint, plus easy access to town, a truly great marina, down-home people with some quirky yet charming habits, and plenty of places to satisfy the inner boater have made Crisfield one of the Bay's favorite destinations.

So Skippy, Hal and I were fairly humming in anticipation. (Actually, Skippy is fairly humming to be on his way anywhere, so he doesn't count.) There was only one issue that threw a shadow over our happy project. Were we too late? Had Crisfield already gone from quaint to wall-to-wall condo? That was certainly the talk I'd heard from Solomons to Salisbury: It's all over, they said, they're building condominiums in Crisfield! Or, alternately: They're building all these condominiums in Crisfield, but I wonder who's going to live there? If you can't find blue cheese or a good dry cleaner anywhere in town you may not be able to sell condominiums.

That last comment came in a round-about way from Whitey Schmidt, a 10-year Crisfield come-here and cookbook author with a title of his own, the Blue Crab Guru. I had called him when I decided to make Crisfield my first landing site of the season. "They have started building a few highrises wherever there's waterfront and a view," he confirmed. "So, it's beginning. New life is coming to Crisfield." Crisfield is a quiet town now, he continued, but once there were a hundred or more oyster-shucking houses at the dock; now there is one. Terrapin soup was found in every restaurant in America; now we don't eat terrapin. The trains are gone, and a lot of the fishing industry has left. So, all things considered, Schmidt says, the condos may be a move in the right direction. "Besides, someday you might even be able to buy blue cheese in Crisfield."

But were recreational boaters and other tourists going to be happy about the Crisfield come-heres, or at least with their outward and visible sign: condominiums? I threw off that shadow as Solomons Lump light passed to starboard and I started listening for the bell at green "5". Pretty soon we would turn to head south in Hal's 17-foot cutty until we reached the entrance of the Little Annemesex channel to Crisfield and Somers Cove Marina.

Somers Cove is definitely one of the big attractions for boaters visiting Crisfield. With more than 400 slips and famously easy to maneuver around, there is nearly always plenty of room for everyone. The marina was built in the late 1950s, while Crisfield's favorite son, J. Millard Tawes was governor of Maryland. The state still owns and maintains it and, over the years, has expanded its slips and facilities. The marina is now also the site of the J. Millard Tawes Museum and Visitors Center. And it was here that Hal and I made our first stop, after tying up at a transient slip and arranging for the ship's dog to cool his heels with a big bowl of water and a bully stick in the shade of the nearby picnic pavilion.

The museum is a great place to get a handle on Crisfield's history. If you can do it, be sure to take Crisfield Heritage Foundation curator Tim Howard's walking tour, which leaves the museum every morning at 10. Thanks to the fog, we didn't manage to make it, but it's going to be a prime motivation for my next visit to Crisfield. Howard, a Crisfield native, has an enthusiasm for the town and for history with a capital *H*

*The sun sets over the Bay and Crisfield's public dock.*
*Preceding pages: The walkway along Crisfield's largest marina, Somers Cove. [Photographs courtesy of Crisfield City Hall.]*

running deep in his veins. Like so many men in Crisfield, his beginnings are inseparable from the water and the seafood industry, but like so many men in Crisfield he has been forced to look elsewhere for a living. In Howard's case, he went back to school and discovered history. He returned to Crisfield and began volunteering at the museum. When the opportunity for a paying job turned up, he jumped at it. Now he leads tours, works on the foundation's new Cedar Marsh Wildlife Preserve—which will soon have a new kayak trail—and changes lightbulbs, as needed. He also works with legions of school groups that come through, the dozen Elderhostel programs the foundation hosts each year and now cruise ships.

"Cruise ships?" I exclaimed.

"Two years ago there were none," Howard explained, "last year there were a couple, and this summer there will be eight to ten cruise boats stopping at Crisfield." He left to take a call from the Mariners Museum in Newport News, Va., as foundation director Chris Tyler came in. "They are calling to confirm arrangements for an Elderhostel cruise that will leave from there and will stop here," she said, before also leaving to field a call.

"Many of these cruises ships are Americana Cruise Line ships and were built right next door in Salisbury," Tim Howard said when he returned. The foundation, he explained, arranges programs for the cruise passengers, including trips to nearby Smith and Tangier islands. Some cruises are birding excursions and some geared toward history.

After perusing the museum and its exhibits, which range from arrowheads to all manner of maritime artifacts (including some decoys by Crisfield's world famous artists in wood, the Ward brothers), Hal and I retrieved the ship's dog and strolled into town. Meandering through the residential areas, we saw relic after elegant relic of oyster prosperity: many dozens of Victorian homes in varying states of both decay and restoration. "They represent the oyster money of the 1920s and thirties," Howard had told us. The brick ranchers on the fringes of town, he said, were built by crab money in the 1950s and '60s.

Howard's voice continued to echo in our ears as we made our first stop downtown, slipping into Goodsell Alley near the city dock for ice cream and a hands-on approach to history. "If you actually put your hand on the old oyster house, you can feel the rough [cinder] blocks it was built with," Howard had said as he told us about the tour we were not going to get. "Then you can put your hands on the next building, where the ice-cream shop is, and feel the smooth blocks. You can feel the difference in time." So Hal and I did that, while Skipper did something else I don't want to get too specific about. Then we docked the ship's dog at a post outside and went in to get some ice cream. The purveyor of ice cream came back out with us, carrying a bowl of water for the dog. With all hands happy, we decided to get a better look at the old oyster house. MeTompkins is one of only a few seafood houses still operating in Crisfield. We walked between its two buildings, the larger of which lies in the shadow of a block of condominiums. To the left, out on the old dock, sat a wrecked car, with an oyster boat tied up next to it. I would have asked, but saw no one to tell me the story.

Goodsell Alley itself could tell a few tales. Late in the 19th century, during the heyday of the oyster trade and when Crisfield was the second largest city in Maryland, Goodsell Alley was the home to bars and bawdy houses, not demure ice-cream parlors. To deal with the ramifications of this new rip-roaring lifestyle, Crisfield established its first police force in 1872. I mention this particularly so that I can share that the town's second police chief was named John S. "Pigtail" Sterling. Its third: Isaac T. "Scapper" Powell. Things must have calmed down after that, because the nicknames seem to end there. (You can find the names of all the police chiefs as well as many other bits of information in *Crisfield, Maryland, 1676–1976*, an endlessly fascinating and thoroughly opinionated 1977 book by Woodrow T. Wilson—no relation. Wilson, a Crisfield native and retired career Army officer, wrote three books on his beloved hometown, this last to celebrate its bicentennial.)

---

Hal, Skippy and I retraced our steps and turned right to the city dock, still very much the center of activity for Crisfield residents and visitors alike. This is where you go to find the boats headed for Tangier and Smith islands. This is also where you go to find people waiting for boats, watching boats, catching up on news. And what was the center of attraction on this day? A cruise ship! Yes, tied up alongside of the dock was a three-deck passenger ship of about 200 feet. And it was creating a certain quiet stir among Crisfielders, who in any case keep a close eye on all things maritime. It was hard to tell which was greater—the cruise ship passengers' curiosity for Crisfield, or Crisfield's curiosity for them. I was pretty interested in both, myself. I stopped to chat with a woman sitting in a car parked just where the dock turns into the two-tiered city pier—

or the sunset viewing stand, as Whitey Schmidt calls it. She told me she had sent her husband up the dock to find out what the ship was. In the time it took to confirm that she was a born Crisfielder and that she and her husband come down regularly to watch the boats, he returned with a brochure. American Canadian Caribbean Line. Two- and three-week tours up and down the Bay and the East Coast. He was ready to sign up, his wife was not. Getting on a boat to visit her sister on Tangier Island was more than enough seafaring for her, she said. What did she think of the condominiums, I asked her. "Crisfield is changing," she replied. "We natives don't see it yet, but it will be good in the end."

That Crisfield is changing seems to be accepted wisdom all around. Sterling & Son Hardware offers a good example. That business, which began in the 19th century as a tin shop, has already made plans to change with the times. It was Skippy's idea that we stop in. We had just spent a few minutes admiring the wide blue beauty of Tangier Sound from the sunset pier and had started walking uptown when the store's open door, the cool shade and the happy odor of hardware and marine supplies drew Skippy in. "He's welcome to come in," Susan Sterling and Karin Schneider

*A aerial view of Crisfield, Md. [Photograph courtesy of Crisfield City Hall.]*

called out, encouraging his trespass. I followed suit, while Hal wandered up the street. The store, actually two stores—one predominantly hardware and the other marine supplies—is planning some changes to meet what is expected to be a wider market in recreational boaters, Sterling told us. "We will be carrying more recreational boating supplies," she said. "Perhaps the store will be divided into a part for watermen and part for recreational boaters." (The urge to protect the watermen is a determined counterpoint to Crisfield's acknowledgement of the need for change—or at least its inevitability.) At the hardware store, Sterling said, there are plans to add polo shirts and other leisure items, "kind of the softer side of hardware."

Skippy was ready to spend a lot more time with his new friends, but we still had something of a hike before we got up to Crisfield's main business section. When most of the town as it exists today was built, the oyster houses and other seafood plants crowded around the docks, many built on pilings over the marsh that separated the land from the water so that the boats could offload directly to the plants. In time, the plants' tons of discarded oyster shells filled in the marsh to make dry land. That left the main part of town strung out at a diagonal to the highway—and, far more importantly at the time, the railroad, which ran right down to the docks.

It was the railway that gave Crisfield its name—the one it has now—and assured its position as seafood capital of the world, because it was able to hustle fresh oysters, crabs and, for a brief time, terrapins to major markets from Baltimore to the nation beyond. John W. Crisfield, an officer with the Eastern Shore Railroad, had seen the importance of the project and had pushed for the extension of the line. The railhead was named Crisfield in his honor and, soon, so was the town. Its earliest European name had been Annemesex Neck, for the local Indian tribe, and was founded as an English town in 1666 by Benjamin Summers. Its port was called Somers Cove (spelling was an inexact science back then), and eventually, since nearly all its comings and goings were maritime, that became the town's name—until Crisfield came along. Somers Cove lives on, of course, as the marina, and the Indian word survives in the Big and Little Annemesex rivers. The tribe, alas, does not.

Downtown—or would it be uptown?—Crisfield is an energetic mix of historic architecture, empty storefronts, long-established businesses, discount stores and intriguing upstarts. It is also the home of one of the locals' new favorite restaurants, Mi Pueblito Grill ("It's not just Mexican. They really cook there," Susan Sterling told me. "I've even been served quail.")

Mexican-style quail would have to wait; I had an appointment with the mayor. So Hal and Skippy went off on their own, and I headed for the village offices, which are near the top of Main Street. Two years ago, Mayor Percy Purnell rode into office on a wave of public indignation that brought a record number of voters to the polls, ousting the incumbent mayor and most of the council. Not surprisingly, it had to do with change.

Purnell and his allies objected to a public/private revitalization project that would have been privately funded, but would also, Purnell said, have given the private interest too much control. And, yes, condominiums were an underlying element. It was four years ago that the first condominiums were built, Purnell continued, and before the election more than 400 new units had been approved. Not that the new mayor opposes condominiums. "Condos are not a bad thing," he said, "they improve the tax base and allow the city to do things it wouldn't otherwise be able to. Would I have done it? Perhaps a little differently."

Purnell is one of Crisfield's many been-here-befores. Twenty years ago, he was mayor. Then he moved away to work. Recently he returned and ran for council. "All of my best memories center on Crisfield. I feel it needs to be protected. Times are going to change, but it needs to be done so people here won't," Purnell said. With an average annual income of less than $18,000, Crisfield's residents would soon be left behind, he said. The city is just completing a comprehensive plan and is seeking bids for the development of its own revitalization plan, aimed at finding that elusive balance between encouraging growth while preserving a way of life (fishing) that is becoming increasingly untenable. There are also plans for trying to help watermen with legislation. One of them is to make sure that the Small Boat Harbor stays in their hands. If passed, the ordinance would allow those recreational boaters who now own docks in the harbor to keep them, but when they do sell, it must be to someone in the marine industry.

---

Skippy and Hal were just coming back down Main Street when I stepped out of the mayor's office. "Go scout out the perfect place for dinner, while I make one last stop," I called out, ducking into Heart of the Home Fine Foods. Whitey Schmidt had suggested that I talk with its proprietor, Susan Linyear. "She's part of the good change that's coming," Schmidt had said. The shop certainly looked like a change for Crisfield.

Coffees, teas, specialty foods. Cheese. Hmmm, I thought, I think I see what's coming.

Linyear is definitely a Crisfield come-here. Before she saw an ad for retail space on the internet, she'd never even heard of the place. "I had been a personal chef and caterer for several years, and I was looking for some space in D.C. to open my own shop," Linyear said. "I saw the Crisfield ad and came down to take a look. I loved the ambience of the town, and I absolutely loved the price." She opened Heart of the Home this March. As the weather has warmed up, so has her business. "People are asking for specific things, like apple or vanilla tea, or a particular barbecue seasoning, and this gets my juices going, thinking of things." And cruise ships. Earlier in the day, she and the owner of Debbi's Chocolate and Gift Shop next door, and the owner of the Captain's Galley had put on a demonstration for the passengers of the cruise ship I had seen earlier. Passengers learned to shuck oysters. The local businesses made some sales. Everyone was happy.

"It is small business that is going to grow Crisfield," Linyear said. "A new plant isn't going to open up." So she and other local business owners

The channel into Somers Cove Marina, bound by Crisfield's waterfront condos and H. Glenwood Evans & Sons Seafood docks. [Photograph by Wikimedia Commons/Baldeaglebluff.]

have formed a marketing group to make Crisfield and their businesses better known to recreational boaters and other potential tourists.

And cheese? (I had to ask.) "I will be carrying a variety of new cheeses beginning next month, like feta, goat cheese, blue cheese." Say no more, I said, and ran out to find Hal and Skippy. I felt a sudden urge to check out a few condominium prices before we settled down for dinner.

It only takes one building to alter a skyline, and in Crisfield that deed is already done. More than a dozen additional buildings are on the drawing board, but whether they will ever be completed depends on whether superb views, great fishing, a charming population . . . and blue cheese . . . will be enough to draw come-heres down there. So far the few dozen people who have come have made little impact on the town itself. Then how would I answer my question: Have condos spoiled Crisfield? You'll just have to come on down and judge for yourself.

---

This article first appeared in *Chesapeake Bay Magazine* in July 2007. Jody Argo Schroath is senior editor of the magazine and editor of its annual *Guide to Cruising Chesapeake Bay*.

# Other Publications from Chesapeake Bay Media

## Chesapeake Bay Magazine
### The essential monthly guide to boating on the Bay.
This is the magazine you'll find on every Chesapeake boater's coffee or galley table, offering destination and cruising articles, boating adventures, how-to information, boat reviews, gear and gadgets, Chesapeake culture, history and nature—everything the Bay boater or aficionado wants and needs to know. To subscribe, visit *store.ChesapeakeBoating.net* or call 877-804-8624.

## Guide to Cruising Chesapeake Bay
### The Chesapeake from top to bottom, thoroughly updated annually.
If you're out and about on the Bay, this is the book you need to keep in arm's reach—nearly 400 pages of priceless information and very specific local knowledge about every creek, river and port of call on the vast Chesapeake, with chart segments, maps of waterfront towns, marina listings, restaurant listings, museums, annual events and all essential Bay-specific boater information. To order the current edition, visit *store.ChesapeakeBoating.net* or call 877-804-8624.

## And coming in November 2014. . .

## Destination Chesapeake:15 Great Cruises in Virginia
### The Old Dominion companion to this book!
We didn't stop at the state line; we started a new book! As with this volume, it's our editors' selection of 15 of the best Virginia boating destinations from past issues of *Chesapeake Bay Magazine*—editor T.F. Sayles on Occoquan, senior editor Jody Argo Schroath on Colonial Beach and Urbanna, editor-at-large Wendy Mitman Clarke on Cape Charles and Gwynn's Island, tidewater correspondent Paul Clancy on Fleets Bay and the Lynnhaven River. No lower Bay explorer should be without it! To order a copy, visit *store.ChesapeakeBoating.net* or call 877-804-8624.